Speed Train Your Own Bird Dog

Speed Train
Your Own Bird Dog

Larry Mueller

Stackpole Books

Copyright © 1990 by Larry Mueller

Published by
STACKPOLE BOOKS
5067 Ritter Road
Mechanicsburg, PA 17055-6921
www.stackpolebooks.com

Printed in the United States of America

20 19 18 17 16 15 14 13

First Edition

Library of Congress Cataloging-in-Publication Data

Mueller, Larry.
   Speed train your own bird dog / Larry Mueller.
      p.   cm.
   ISBN 0-8117-2304-6
   1. Bird dogs—Training. I. Title.
SF428.5.M833   1990
636.7'52—dc20   89-39933
                                                                  CIP

ISBN 978-0-8117-2304-6

To the wonders of grandchildren. We see ourselves in them — but vastly improved. Margie, Rachel, Jesse, Melissa, Mat, Adam, and Noel are even more fun than bird dogs.

Contents

Part 1

The Super-Speed-Train Period

Before You Start

Speed Train Your Own Bird Dog, like *Speed Train Your Own Retriever*, explains a system of teaching methods selected for their ability to swiftly get your dog's attention and understanding. Some of these methods are old, yet remain the most effective; some are new and innovative. All are described in a sequence designed to help the busy amateur train his dog with the least intrusion on his time. You can train your dog as much or as little as you like. The idea of the Speed-Train system is to get you the dog you want without a fight, and without long, hard hours of work. If you find yourself turning red and yelling, stop right there. Read that section again. Perhaps you've misunderstood some of the descriptions. Followed consistently, and in a timely manner, the Speed-Train program is, and *must be* if it is to work effectively, a fun time with your dog.

One sentence of caution: Dogs learn so quickly and easily with some of these training methods that you may be inclined to believe "they know it now." That's not how the canine mind works. An adult human may learn something permanently in one lesson, but dogs are less intelligent than children. And like small children, they may easily understand the lesson but it takes practice to keep the lesson from being forgotten. Also, no two dogs are alike. We'll compensate for this as we go.

A second word of caution: Do not buy several books on bird dog training and then pick and choose the methods you like from each. You'll cobble up the sequence and timing. Use this book or another, but use only one. By the same token, do not take this book to a professional trainer and ask what he thinks of this or that. He'll be inclined to say, "Aw, no, what I do is . . ." And if you go to a second pro, you'll get a second, but different, "What I do is . . ." If you're going to do the training yourself, use the book.

When I wrote the retriever book, I predicted that pros might scoff at the number of aids and gadgets we use. That was not meant to be criticism of others. That was the simple recognition of how the human critter, especially an expert, functions. Go to a second doctor and he'll give you a second opinion. Sure enough, some pros, although not as many as I expected, did condemn my use of tools, mostly on the grounds that they aren't needed.

Those pros have the space to train, so they prefer to stick to the old ways, which have worked for them. Fine. But they failed to understand that the amateur has a different set of needs. The amateur doesn't have either the space or the practiced expertise. The training aids compensate for this by allowing him to do most of the training on a small area, often the backyard, and more important, by giving him control when he might otherwise lose it due to lack of experience.

With the cautions out of the way, let's start using the book. As you begin to read, note that the photographs serve an important function. They help explain and clarify the instruction. And they are precisely located so you can use them when referring back to the text. Most training books are difficult and annoying

Nothing is so promising as a springtime pup, and that is true regardless of breed. I have chosen English setters for illustrations because their color reproduces on the printed page better than some of the darker breeds, but of course this book is written for training all breeds of bird dogs.

because you read the text ahead of time. Then, when training begins and you need to look up specific instructions, you have to wade through page after page to find them. Our pictures are placed right ahead of the text they illustrate. It's almost like the text is a long caption for the picture. When you need to find the appropriate step in training, look it up first in the table of contents, then glance at the pictures to zero in swiftly on the training move you need to know more about.

One other thing . . . my use of English setters in most of the photographs does not mean that this book is intended only for setter training. It simply means that English setters look good in pictures. Using one breed also lends a certain continuity to the book. I want to make it very clear that nothing else is implied; I haven't met a bird-dog breed I didn't like.

Step 1

Which Pup

I hope you're reading this before you have your puppy because, despite what you may have heard, there are precise ways to pick the right dog. Picking the right pup is the most important step in training. Training can vary from a breeze to impossible; it will all depend on the pup. Some people say, "Close your eyes and grab." That works only if every dog in the litter is good. One top trainer says let everybody else have first pick. He'll train what's left and make it a champion. That works if you're one of the world's best trainers and have a good litter. Believe me, there are more bad litters than good out there, so you and I need all the help we can get in making the right choice.

When pups released from the kennel rush over to become spectators at the pheasant pen, you're onto something very promising.

Choose any breed of bird dog you want, but keep in mind that there is one absolute: This pup must point. All else is secondary. You may tolerate a dog that can't trail a crippled bird. You might pick up your own birds if the dog doesn't retrieve. A bird dog that doesn't point, however, is as useless as a skiff on the Sahara. A pup can not be taught to be interested in birds and point. It's an instinct that must be in the dog's genes.

When you go to look at a 7 or 8-week-old litter, arrange a time early in the day, if possible, when the pups are most likely to be energetic. Ask to see them running free in the yard. If the breeder has birds, and the pups run over to watch and admire them, you know you're onto something worthwhile. If there are no birds, don't worry. There's a sure way to guarantee that your pup will point.

Never buy a pup eight weeks or older that won't point a rag.

Take along a short pole or fishing rod that has a slightly shorter piece of string attached to its end. Tie a rag to the cord, single out a pup and dance the rag in front of him. When the puppy tries to catch it, flip the rag several feet forward or to the side and let it fall to the ground. If the pointing instinct is very strong, he may walk a step or two toward the rag and lock up like a statue. If instead he races out to catch the rag, give it another flip just before he gets there. Continue to play the game until he points or proves to you that he won't.

The technique for pointing a rag is simple. "Fly" the rag past the pup's line of vision, and let it drop a few feet away. If he chases instead of pointing, flip it away and let it "land" in another location. Continue this until he points or until you're satisfied that he won't.

It's entirely possible that pups won't point when they're tired from playing or sluggish from eating. If the breeder insists that his pups usually do point, arrange another visit for a better time of day. *Never buy a pup that won't point a rag.* If you follow that rule, your pup can't be a total loss. Equally important, you'll have a pup that can begin his training at the absolute best time of life for it—right now—at 7 or 8 weeks old.

Trainers have used bird wings or large feathers to test pups more often than they have cloth. I don't recommend it. A pup's mind is nearly a blank page at this point. He has had few significant experiences to clutter his brain and interfere with recollection. In my experience, what is learned early lasts for life. The pup will sight-point either a wing or rag. The wing smells like bird; the rag does not. At this young age the pup should not make an association between sight pointing and the smell of bird. I do not want the pup who later smells a bird to think he must get close enough to see it before he points.

One experience may not cause sight pointing. Who, though, can resist showing off the pup's pointing ability for the wife and kids? After that, every friend who shows up will have to see the trick. And who knows exactly how many times it takes to lock in sight pointing for life. This is a Speed-Train system. We're using methods that quickly get the dog's attention; *we avoid possible mistakes that take precious time to correct.*

OK, you'll make sure the pup points, you'll use a rag instead of a wing, and you won't overdo sight pointing.

But wait! Don't carry off the first pup that points. Maybe all the pups in this litter point. You can, and should, be even more selective. You might drive the breeder nuts, but that goes with the turf. You are going to live with this dog.

There are dominant and submissive dogs. Maybe you think, "Boy! I want a bold, dominant dog, just like me!" Well, maybe you really don't. The dominant dog has the nature to lead the pack, not follow. He'll try to train *you*. He'll test your authority at every opportunity. Training will never end because he's always sure his ways make more sense than yours.

The submissive dog can be just as bold in the field as a dominant dog. They just aren't as pushy with their pack leader. They're happy to be led, so they're comfortable dogs to be around and to train.

The pecking order begins to establish itself in a litter when the puppies are 7 weeks. The older the pups are, the easier it is to see the difference in their assertiveness. Watch them carefully and, if possible, watch them on more than one occasion. There are dominant males and dominant females. Most often, the dominant male is the biggest and the dominant female is the noisiest. If you can pick out those two in the litter, you'll notice they're troublemakers, often provoking fights to prove their dominance.

At the other end of the pecking order, if it has become established, is the underdog, the timid little fellow keeping off to himself to avoid conflict. Avoid this pup, too, because he is submissive and shy.

Once you have the timid and dominant pups culled, the next step is to find a pup that's submissive, yet intelligently bold. Are the other puppies curious about their surroundings? Will they approach you willingly, yet cautiously? Do they actively investigate their surroundings when running free in the yard?

When you decide which pups are doing these things, get ready to make a loud noise near them. If they're very close to a metal shed, rap the side of it with the back of your fist. Or bang a couple of metal buckets together. Go equipped to make such a noise in case nothing is handy at the kennel.

The surprise of the loud noise should send all of the pups dashing toward Mama. To not be spooked into flight would indicate definite lack of intelligence. OK, so the intelligent dogs run. Now watch how far. Those that are intelligently bold will run a short distance, then turn around to see what caused that racket.

If you have eliminated the obviously dominant individuals, dismissed the timid ones, and have found an intelligently bold pup among those that point the rag, your job as a trainer has been reduced to a fraction of what it might have been.

Maybe you're even more fortunate and find that several pups qualify. What now! I know what's about to happen. You're ready to reach for the pup that's marked or colored like Uncle Joe's ol' Neverfail, the best dog you ever saw. Wait. Ability is between the ears, not on the coat. Watch a while longer. Maybe one or more of these pups have retrieving instincts. Have you noticed any carrying sticks around? That's the first manifestation of the retrieving instinct. If they haven't been carrying anything, try the pups one at a time in the yard. Toss a knotted sock, or throw a tennis ball within a couple feet of a pup. Does he chase and carry it? That's great in itself. If one of those little pups fetches it back to you, though, *buy him.* If there's still a choice of several pups that do everything right, now pick for pretty. It can't hurt to enjoy the sight of your dog.

If you want to be really scientific, and the breeder will allow further intrusion on his time (paying him extra for a choice pup might improve his hospitality), contact Dr. Larry Myers, a professor of veterinary medicine at Auburn University. Myers has developed a kit to test whether a dog—a puppy or adult—has a poor, average, above average, or superior sense of smell. (Write to Dr. Larry Myers, Myers/Brown-Myers, 674 Meadowbrook Drive, Auburn, Alabama 36830.) Sometimes a dog with an average nose, but great bird desire, can be a better hunter than a dog with a superior nose and little desire. Obviously, however, you don't want a pup with an inferior nose.

Now that you know how to pick a pup, some of you will remember that the breed, breeder, or bloodline that you want a pup from is a thousand miles away. The pup will have to be shipped air freight. How do you pick a pup from a litter you can't see?

You can't. You can, however, tell the breeder what you'd like him to look for. The one thing you can insist on is that the pup is already pointing and will point within two weeks of arriving at your house. It may take that long for the little fellow to become accustomed to his new home and overcome the shock of separation from his mother and littermates. An honest breeder should be willing to guarantee in writing that the pup will point as agreed upon, or he'll refund the purchase price and accept return freight charges.

Important: Avoid show-bred stock like the plague. Show breeders will argue that it makes sense to select dogs physically assembled to move well in the field. What they don't understand is that you can't select for that trait only, or even first, and get a good hunter. In fact, the dog with bred-in ability and desire can have terrible physical conformation and still provide a wonderful day of hunting. On the other hand, a dog without strong bird interest will loaf and play through the day no matter how perfect his build.

Good idea: If possible, read all of part 1 before getting the pup. Know what training aids you'll need and send for the catalogs listed in the appendix, so you'll know where to acquire those items.

Step 2

Time to Start

You've just returned home with *one* 7 or 8-week-old pup that points. Not two. Two pups will give each other more attention than they give you, and you'll never have enough time and patience to train both. I also hope you were able to follow my instructions on selecting a submissive pup with bold intelligence. If so, you are set up to easily achieve training that no pro can accomplish. Don't fool around; you have no more than eight weeks to do initial training.

This two-month period, when a pup is 8 to 16 weeks old compares to what I call the "wanting to wash dishes" stage in children. From about 3 to 6 years old, children regard you as an all-knowing superior being. They want nothing more than to be with you, to do what you do, and to be exactly like you. Of course, just as soon as they're old enough and really can "wash the dishes," they've outgrown the stage. They have their own ideas about what they'd rather do and how it should be done.

Dr. Maria Montessori, born in 1870 in Rome, recognized this tremendous willingness of children in this age group to absorb information. This eagerness in children is, in fact, almost mind-boggling. They're learning an entire language during that period in addition to who knows how many cultural rules and values. Dr. Montessori devised a system of schooling to take advantage of that incredible stage in life.

I learned of Montessori School by default. My wife Micky and I were babysitting for our granddaughter Rachel whenever both of her parents were working. Our daughter Mary became annoyed at me for not correcting Rachel. (Frankly, I didn't know of anything Rachel did wrong, or I might have corrected her.) Nevertheless, Mary went looking for more responsible supervision and found a Montessori School. By age 4, Rachel was sounding out words on store fronts. At 5, the summer before entering first grade, she read more than 50 children's books from the library. At 12, she was having a bit of trouble with algebra, so Rachel and I spent part of about four evenings on the basics. Suddenly, she squealed with delight. "Grandpa! I understand!" From that moment she was solving equations. Montessori School taught Rachel at the right age that learning is fun and rewarding, and her enthusiasm for discovery has never diminished.

Gradually, I began to realize that puppies also go through a very similar intense period of learning, although for a much briefer time. By the time I was helping Rachel with algebra, I knew that when learning is made rewarding during that blank-page phase of a child's or puppy's mind, the love of learning is permanent. In addition, all those things which children and puppies learn in that period – because those things were made so highly rewarding – are loved for life.

Understand me clearly, however. *You can not drill anything into puppies or children at that stage.* Try it and they fold on you. Raise your voice and it's over. Threaten or punish, and they learn about as fast as a fence post. Make it pay big dividends, however, and they catch on instantly. Furthermore, they never forget it.

You can't hire a professional trainer to do this for the same reason most children don't go to Montessori School. The majority of us either can't afford it or aren't willing to pay for it. In addition, dog trainers want a year-old dog that can stand the pressure and advance at a fairly rapid pace in order to please the owner. That fact brings up another important reason why the owner should teach his own pup.

There was a time when owners told trainers, "Try this dog for a month. Send me a bill for the next month if he's worth training. Otherwise, send me the collar." The pro then embarked on a program of tough do-it-or-else training. The good dogs survived. It was bad news for poor quality individuals, but the culling did improve the breeds.

Most pros haven't greatly changed their tactics. There are still few behavioral trainers around. Owners though, have changed. Many act as if they've made an adoption, not bought a pup. If the pup is too soft to take professional training, or if he caves in because he isn't bright enough to catch on readily, the owner feels stuck with the dog for life.

This same dog under owner training will seldom be a great hunter, but he won't be worthless either, if the owner starts as early as directed.

You'll make the effort? Fine. Now place your hand on the Bible, and repeat after me: "I will not lose my temper. I will not expect more of my pup than I would a baby. The next two months will be nothing but fun for both pup and me. *And if it isn't fun for me, I'll never let my pup know it!*"

Let's start with where you've decided to keep the pup. The worst place is with an older dog that will quickly assume the role of pack leader, which is a role reserved for you. The next worst place is with another pup. Although both may regard you as boss, they'll be too busy playing with each other to give you much attention. A little better—mighty little—is alone in a kennel run. In this situation, most pups enjoy scant association with their owners. As a result, many pups become shy, darting for the safety of their house when people do come around. For whatever reason, few owners enter the run, go to the dog house, and insist that the dog be sociable.

It's far better for the young pup to be on a chain than in a kennel. There's nowhere to hide but the dog house, and he's easy to pull out of there with the chain. Better yet is a 20-foot-long ground cable tie-out that he can run up and down on with the chain. It gives him more freedom, but he must still be sociable.

Best of all is in the house with you. The old tale still persists that hunting dogs shouldn't be pets. This is absolute foolishness. The dog can't learn to respond to your wishes while it's outside and you're in the house. Living with you greatly speeds the dog's willingness to accept you as pack leader.

If you can't keep the pup inside, I understand. I can't, either. I've always had too many dogs of various types and breeds—usually eight to twelve—to keep them in the house. The havoc and odor would be unbearable. (And not everybody wants even one dog in the house for the same reasons.) So don't apologize.

If the pup will live with you, he'll have to be potty trained. The airline carrier he was shipped in is your best tool. Buy a cage or carrier if you bought the pup locally. Place it where you'll want the dog's bed to permanently remain. He'll have to spend much of his time in that carrier, but don't feel cruel. Your pup will learn to regard this cage as his domain, his private quiet place, and his refuge or safe place. Further, and this is important, make sure every

The key to early training is making it all rewards and successes, but *never* pressure. Here, because I have nothing else handy, the pup is accepting spit on my hand as a reward. It is a natural way to help form the pack leader relationship with a pup, because canine pups, under natural circumstances, accept saliva-coated food from the dam and other superior members of the pack.

member of the family understands that they must respect this safe place. When the dog gets into trouble and races to his safe place, that's the end of it. He's home safe. No further punishment. This is essential for his psychological development. We want a bold, self-confident bird dog, not a wimp inhibited for life because there is no refuge from wrath. His "safe house" will not interfere with obedience later.

Confining a puppy to the carrier or cage works so well in potty training because dogs do not willingly dirty their own nests. If you time it well, and do not ignore the pup beyond the time he can hold it, there will be few accidents.

As soon as you're awake, take the pup to a corner of the yard acceptable to you as his permanent potty place. If possible, locate it on a straight line directly from your back door. Better yet, make it a straight line from the cage through the door to the spot. He'll learn much quicker if the route is uncomplicated.

Feed the pup at exactly the same times morning and evening. Supply water at the same time. Soon after eating, the pup will relieve himself. Have him outside at the right spot. You'll quickly learn how many minutes elapse between eating and pottying and, therefore, when to let him out. When the pup has learned where to go (they quickly learn to sniff for their own odor, and then hate to break in new places) water can be made readily available. He'll let you know when he needs to go out. When the pup matures, he can be fed once a day.

Most pups cry during the first few nights they're away from their littermates. If that's a problem, try wrapping an alarm clock in a towel and placing it in his cage at night. The ticking seems to quiet pups by replacing the heartbeat sounds of mother and siblings.

Point to ponder: Change is hard to accept. If friends start scoffing at you for trying to train a baby dog, consider this: If 8 months to a year is the best, most natural time to begin training a canine mind, why do coyote pups start going along on short hunts with their mamas at 8 weeks?

Step 3

Leash, Collar, and Name

You probably picked a name for the pup before you brought it home. If not, do so immediately, because the two-month period of important early training will be gone before you know it.

We're told to choose one-syllable names for dogs because they're too stupid to recognize longer names. Don't believe it. I know a slow-witted old hound called Buford. He knows his name. So did Goforth. I named my latest pup Buckshot because his freckles were too big to call him Birdshot. He learned his name in one lesson. I said the word as I handed him a big piece of baked chicken skin.

There's nothing wrong with one-syllable names, of course. It does pay to choose a name that makes a good sharp command. Blitz cuts the air with a certain force. When I call, "Buck*shot*," his ears come straight up, and he's on his way.

Don't let the dog be named Snookums, or some such sweet sounding term of endearment. "Snookums, come," may bring more than a few raised eyebrows and chuckles from friends in the field.

Provide Buckshot with a collar big enough to grow into, and frequently check that it's loose enough to slide two fingers under it with ease.

As soon as the pup settles into his new home — it takes a day or so — provide him with a collar. Buckle it snug enough that he can't slip out of it and loose enough so two of your fingers fit under it. Pups grow fast, so check the collar frequently. One time I made the mistake of giving a pup to a careless young man. Stopping to visit, I found the neglected pup on a chain, a pained look in his eyes, and a strange odor around his head. I discovered the collar was so tight that hair and hide were gone. Imagine being tied by a collar digging into bare, festering flesh? The dog went home with me at that moment.

The pup won't like his new collar. It seems as unnatural to him as a first haircut does to a child. Don't worry about it. He'll scratch at it until he realizes it won't come off, then he'll forget it.

Dragging a yard of check cord is the first step toward leash training, and it requires none of your time.

He won't care for a yard of cord, either, but attach that to the collar. Let him drag it around. Finally, he'll probably play with it. Long before the day is over, he'll accept both collar and cord as part of life.

Full leash control is also taught on the pup's own time, not yours.

The next day, tie the pup's cord to his carrier, the fence of his kennel, a tree, or whatever is handy, for about 15 minutes. He'll fight it, complaining bitterly, but he'll settle down. If he chews on the cord replace it with a light chain.

The next day, add five more minutes to the cord training. Continue adding time each day until the pup accepts tethering without a fight. At that point, presto! Without all the annoying struggles on your part, the pup has learned leash control and acceptance. Better yet, he has learned it on his time; not yours.

Important: Do not neglect this simple leash training. It is important to later off-leash control as well as leash and check cord acceptance right now.

Step 4

Freedom Trains

During certain aspects of a pup's mental development, allowing him freedom trains him more quickly than anything else you could do. Some historians say slaves, even when freed, were at an enormous disadvantage because the plantation had been their whole world. They had no idea what to expect beyond its borders. I'm sure this was true because I see much the same thing with pups that grow up in kennels. The busy or procrastinating owner doesn't make time to be with his young dog. Suddenly, it's hunting season. For perhaps the first time, the dog is taken to the field. He's excited, but fearful, with his tail down, hanging close to his master who is getting angrier by the minute because he's embarrassed that his dog would be so timid. Of course the dog is timid. Solitary confinement in his kennel during his formative months has taught him that the world is perhaps 4-by-12 feet and that the major events of life are eating, relieving oneself, and barking at the neighbor's cat.

The pup that gets out for training once, twice, or three times a week is much better prepared for the field. The pup that is kept in the house and gets outside for training, is vastly more prepared because his mental growth advances rapidly during association with the family. Nothing, absolutely nothing, however, develops the mind of a very small pup better than running free.

Freedom expands the puppy's mind while kennel confinement stifles it. Let the pup join in on all possible activities.

Running free, the pup learns what's dangerous, what's not, and how to negotiate with the world, including a multitude of little things such as drinking from a hydrant. This pup will not fear new experiences.

If you live in the country and back from the road, you're among the few blessed with the ideal place to start a pup. Just put him outside in the morning, unsnap the chain, or open the kennel. Let him do what he will, and he'll immediately begin to investigate the world, gradually increasing his boundaries, just as children do. Every time you, or a member of the family, goes outside, he will come running. A few pages from now, you'll see how we take advantage of this in a variety of ways to achieve almost instant training.

Those of you who don't live in the country may balk at this idea. Give it serious thought; don't dismiss it. This important period of development lasts for just these two months. Giving a pup freedom is *so* important that I would fence in my backyard just for that purpose. That's still not like total freedom around a country home, but it's an enormous help. If nicely constructed, the fence could be an attractive addition, and it will always be useful for confining dogs and perhaps little children. If I couldn't afford a fence, or if the neighbors frowned on permanent fences, I'd make it temporary. Tell the neighbors what you're doing so they won't be disturbed. It will only be up for a couple of months. Use steel fence posts and 4-foot-high chicken wire and fence as much ground as possible. It's a good idea to fold the bottom foot of wire inward to prevent the pup from digging underneath it and escaping.

Buckshot will practice his stock in trade – pointing – on butterflies, bees, houseflies, sparrows, and anything else with wings.

In the country, some properly trained dogs can run free all their lives, never taking off to hunt unless you come out with the gun. That makes dog ownership a special delight. A permanently fenced backyard comes closest to this. When a country dog starts self-hunting, or when his roaming causes trouble with the neighbors, total freedom must end. Long before that, however, the very important early training is accomplished.

Step 5

Awakening Pup's Nose

The rate at which the pup learns from this point on, especially if he's running free, will make your head swim. I'll explain each step one at a time, but you'll be doing all of them rather simultaneously during this period. When you actually do each step simply depends upon opportunity. You will be taking advantage of what comes naturally for the pup, and reinforcing correct behavior by making the pup believe that it pays big dividends. This important training will cost you almost no extra time.

Remember how I taught Buckshot his name in one lesson? Well, no matter how quickly they catch on, dogs don't remember very long without reinforcement. So, every time I went outside after that, I'd take along a table scrap and call "Buckshot, COME."

Later on, I deliberately neglected to have a goody perhaps every third or fourth time. Instead, I'd substitute an excited greeting as he'd come running, then follow it with lots of hugs, petting, and enthusiastic talk about what a beautiful, intelligent puppy he is. Buckshot believed every word of it, as all puppies do, and he has never failed to respond to his name. In addition, he had instantly learned a bird dog's second most important command – COME. It was just a matter of continuing to call it with his name.

The crucial nose awakening is easily begun by dragging a chunk of leftover meat, skin, or fat about six feet through the grass.

One thing I'm finding increasingly important is early awakening of the pup's nose. It seems the average owner thinks a dog's nose is automatic. The dog is equipped to read things from scent that are not given to us to know, so we assume he will always use that nose to his best advantage. Not so. I have seen many dogs use their noses poorly. In fact, I'd say most dogs use their noses poorly. I know the reason, too. It's because those dogs spend most of a year loafing in a kennel run before they're exposed to any situation where a sense of smell is required. Kennel living and postponed training only teaches dogs that life means killing time between meals.

Of course a few dogs simply have poor noses. If your pup doesn't seem to catch on to our nose awakening, it would be worth the price of a Myers' nose-testing kit to find out for sure. It's easier to give a pup away as a pet before it's grown, and there's no sense wasting time, effort, and money on a dog with no nose. (See the appendix for the address from which to order a nose kit.)

A pup with a poorer than average nose probably should be discarded. Dr. Myers points out, however, that there's more to hunting than having a good nose. If a dog has great hunting desire and bird interest, he'll perform better than a dog with a superior nose which he doesn't use because he isn't interested.

That's where nose awakening comes in. If the pup is taught at a very early age that using his nose is highly profitable, he will establish good hunting behavior for life. Even if his nose isn't superior, you'll have a valuable hunting dog. And talk about Speed Training! Nose awakening is instantaneous in most pups. And because they're so motivated, almost all pups advance to higher levels of problem solving with nearly 100 percent success rates along the way.

You're already teaching . . . what's his name? . . . shall we call him Buck-shot, too? You're already teaching little Buckshot to come when called. The reward is chicken skin, steak fat, or something else more exciting than dog food, but not a bone. Now expand upon this idea. You may have to tie or kennel the little fellow so he won't see what you're doing. Mark a spot so you can bring the pup right back to it. Drag the goody from that spot through the grass into the wind to another marked spot about 6 feet away. Drop the goody at the second spot.

Free Buckshot with whichever hand doesn't smell like the goody so he won't know about it yet. Let him run around a bit in another area. Gradually walk toward the starting point of the little trail you've laid, and call, "Buckshot, COME!"

Bring your goody-smelling fingers to the pup's nose, then down to the drag trail, and quickly withdraw your hand.

Here he comes! As he arrives, squat down, bringing your goody-smelling fingers to his nose. You'll have his attention. Immediately move your finger the additional foot or so to the beginning of the trail. Place your index finger right on the trail. The instant the pup's nose is right down there with your finger where the trail starts in the grass, quickly withdraw your hand. The odor on the ground will hold the pup's attention. Immediately say, "FIND IT, Buckshot!"

The wind, even if it's just a slight air movement, will be bringing odors directly from the goody to Buckshot, so he'll find it. You can be sure of that. When he does, tell him how proud you are. "Good boy, Buckshot."

You have his attention. When you do this tomorrow, drag the goody DOWNWIND so the pup will *not* be able to air scent it. He'll have to trail it.

Buckshot will trail the drag to his reward, and he'll always associate the FIND IT command with locating something exciting.

Stop and think what you've done. You've added to Buckshot's understanding of his name, you've reinforced his willingness to come on command, and you've awakened serious investigative use of his nose. That's just the beginning, however. You have just introduced trailing which he'll eventually be expected to do on cripples and perhaps running pheasants. In addition, he now understands the command; practice will commit it to lifelong memory. When you drop a bird and point to an area, saying, "FIND IT," he'll know exactly what you want, and regardless whether the bird is found lying where it fell, or must be trailed, Buckshot will know what to do.

As the pup proves his ability to trail the goodies, gradually lengthen the drag with each session. Continue making these trails downwind or crosswind in straight lines until they're about 50 feet long. (You'll make them more complicated later.)

It's not necessary to practice this every day. Two or three times a week is fine – whenever you have special goodies. Don't neglect it. Practice will commit these lessons to your pup's lifelong memory. This is very valuable, very easy training.

Important: If you so much as raise your voice to yell, "No, not over there, you dummy, over here," I'll break your legs. This early puppy training works because it's fun to him, because he is highly motivated by winning *every* time, and because life is wonderful whenever he gets to be with you. You can blow it all with angry shouting or critical sarcasm. If you can control your voice, it's OK to quietly say "noooo" when he slips off of the trail, and just as quietly say "attaboy, Buckshot" when he's close to it. If you can't, simply keep quiet while he works it out. Nose work requires concentration.

Step 6

How to Pet a Dog

A chapter on how to pet a dog? You probably think I'm crazy. Everybody knows how to pet a dog!

Not so. Few people realize it, but there are vastly different ways of petting, and they have an enormous influence over how the dog reacts to you.

One of my daughters was frustrated with a hyperactive dog her family kept in the backyard. Her children couldn't play because the dog was constantly jumping at them, and on them, in a bid for attention. "What can I do?" she pleaded.

I watched how my daughter behaved with the dog. Her petting was a series of quick hand motions roughing up the hair on his shoulder, followed by several quick pats, after which she hoped the dog would go away. Instead of going away, the dog jumped on her excitedly, trying for more.

The dog needed some strong discipline which he promptly received. Then, however, I had to train my daughter on the fine points of petting a dog. Dogs are marvels at responding to people's moods and behaviors, and she was signaling the dog to be hyper by her quick, roughhouse moves.

"If you want a dog to be calm," I said, "pet him slowly. Start at the face and stroke him all the way to the hips. Talk soothingly at the same time. Quick pats will excite him."

The whole family modified their petting habits while I began obedience training with the dog. From that beginning, Melissa, the youngest in the family, and the one who suffered most from Blackjack's jumping, went on to train him to COME, HEEL, SIT, STAY, FETCH, and jump hurdles.

Roughhousing seems like great fun, but it quickly becomes bad news when you're trying to train and all the pup wants to do is wrestle.

When a pup is very small, roughhousing seems like great fun. The pup loves it. He rolls over, and his owner rubs his belly. If the owner is calm and vocally soothing, and if his strokes are slow and quieting, no harm is done. Usually, however, the puppy wants to "play fight." He tries to grab a hand with his mouth. The baby teeth are sharp. So the hand moves farther up the chest and closer to the neck so the teeth can't reach skin. The pup struggles, and the hand goes to the neck under the chin. Paws fly, toenails claw, and the puppy growls. It's amusing to see such a tiny creature thinking he's so tough.

It doesn't take long, however, for play fighting to become a habit. It also doesn't take long before blood is drawn—usually yours—and you realize that the pup has become too big for this sport. Furthermore, it's very difficult to get the dog's attention for serious training when all he wants to do is wrestle.

The best petting for a bird dog is one that will contribute to his most important command: WHOA. When your pup seeks attention, try this: Keep him on his feet with your left hand between his front legs and under his chest while you stroke him from one end to the other with your right hand, softly crooning, "Whooooa."

As the pup grows older, and his personality becomes more established, you may find that he is a bit more timid than you thought. Or maybe you didn't have a choice, and the pup you got is a little shy. Placing him in a somewhat bolder role during petting will sometimes improve his confidence.

Wise petting is soothing instead of agitating.

You're not trying to teach commands now, so don't give orders. Just talk lovingly to the pup while you gently push his rear end down to seat him before you. Then slowly and repeatedly stroke both sides of his muzzle with your hands, going as far back as the corners of his mouth. Wild puppies beg their dams to regurgitate food by licking them under the chin. The same chin licking has remained a fond submissive "me Pup, you Mom" expression among domestic dogs. Our similar petting temporarily makes the timid pup feel like big stuff. It may help embolden a shy pup.

On the other hand, if your pup happens to be a dominant-type, muzzle petting may only further convince him of his dominance. In that case, try petting him into a submissive role. A dog's most strongly submissive expression includes squinted eyes, laid-back ears and short tentative licks. You can't make a dog lick unless he wants to, but you can closely approximate the rest. Seat the dog. With one hand on each side of his face, start with your palms on his cheeks, beginning at the line between his eyes and the corners of his mouth. Wipe back with just enough pressure to pull the skin and cause the eyes to squint. The mouth will pull back too, and that's fine; it's part of what I call the dog's agreeable look. Continue the wiping motion which now pulls the ears back, completing the submissive expression. Hold the expression for a moment as you say "good boy" to the dog.

Repeated regularly, it may help. If you doubt that role playing changes anything, spread a grin across your face. Go ahead. Right now. How do you feel? OK, change it to a frown. Feel different? Of course. If compelled to grin, it's every bit as difficult for you to stay angry as it is for a dog to act dominant with a submissive expression on his face. Feelings follow expressions almost as strongly as expressions follow feelings. I suppose that's why actors who pretend during love scenes so often end up in love with co-stars.

Step 7

No

Teaching NO is such a small thing that it was tempting to include it in another step. NO deserves step status, though, because you must teach it separately during early puppy training. Let me emphasize: *Do not introduce NO during nose awakening, training with food, or in the presence of birds.* While learning NO is essential, all other pup training must be done without a harsh edge in your voice.

If your pup is running free during the day – or living in the house – you won't have to set up anything to teach NO. A puppy gets into things. He'll generate the opportunity for you, probably on his first day at home. It is better, however, to give him a few days to acclimate himself to his new surroundings before teaching NO.

OK, Buckshot has been here say three days and already thinks he owns the place with everybody and everything in it. There he goes with one of your wife's favorite shoes. Grab him! Now what? You can't whip an 8-week-old pup.

You don't have to. Behave just as his dam would, and you'll get through to Buckshot's sensibilities with lightning speed. When he's in the act of mischief (although he doesn't yet know that it's mischief) grab him with your hands by the loose hide on either side of his neck. Say NO loudly, clearly, and as if you mean it while simultaneously and unceremoniously hoisting him off the ground and up to your eye level. With your face right up to his, shake him a little while growling like an angry dog. End the growl with another sharp NO! Stop and stare directly into his eyes. If he's hanging limp in your grip, give another single shake with a simultaneous NO, hold him just a moment more, then put him down. If he's still trying to wiggle out of your grip, instead of hanging limp, repeat with a more thorough shake, growl, and say NO. Stop and see if he's giving up the struggle. If so, one more shake and one more NO, then put him down.

If a pup is running free, you won't have to set up anything to teach NO. He'll soon find a way to make a pest of himself as Buckshot is doing here. He sees me walking Radar, a Tennessee feist (unrefined hunting terrier), and he wants to help.

Buckshot leading Radar is not what I – or the feist – had in mind, but some precocious behavior is too comical to correct.

Attacking Radar because he's getting most of the attention is not simply precocious, however, and it offers an opportunity for NO training.

A very intelligent pup of submissive nature will learn NO in one lesson. Less intelligent pups will take longer, of course. If you have a pup with a dominant nature, especially one that's also not especially brilliant, you'll have to repeat this lesson until the message does get through. With that dog, of course, you won't have to wait long between opportunities for teaching.

Those owners who can't have the puppy in the house or running free will have to set up something. Perhaps use an old slipper. Smear a little gravy or grease somewhere on the edge of the sole or heel for added temptation to speed up the process. Bring Buckshot out of the kennel and let him find the shoe on his own. When he's in the midst of chewing, or even licking the shoe, do the NO training.

To teach NO, grab the pup with both hands by the loose hide on either side of his neck. Pick him up and give him a quick shake as you bark NO! at him. In no way should you inflict real pain during puppy training, but correcting him much the same way his dam would gets immediate understanding.

Should the lesson go unheeded and Buckshot return to his mischief, again act exactly as his dam would. Grab him up more swiftly, shake harder, and absolutely roar the NO in his face. The roar should contain the growl of an outraged dog.

Very important: You are now free to use NO as a correction and you should use it every time the pup tries to jump up, steal objects, chew shoes, and so on. This will keep the command alive in his memory. I repeat, however, do not use NO during the little puppy's training with birds. You'll use it later, but this very early training *must* be ALL fun and games. The pup *must* win in every one of these situations. If you inhibit with punishment, or intimidate with a loud mouth, you'll not only lose the Speed-Train advantage, you'll be worse off than if you had waited to start training until the pup became a year old.

Step 8

Mealtime Come, Heel, and Whoa

You have to feed your dog everyday; twice a day when he's little. Why not take advantage of mealtime and precondition the pup to obedience? Eating is a big event in a dog's life and using it to your advantage takes almost no extra time. With little effort, you can teach your pup the most important words in his vocabulary long before it's time for serious obedience.

To begin teaching COME, squat invitingly, call the command, and offer the pup's food as reward. You have to feed him anyway, so the training costs you no extra time.

Little Buckshot may already know the command COME if you've begun the nose awakening. Whether he knows it or not, call COME when you carry his food outside or walk to the feed barrel with his bowl. He'll quickly learn that COME has perhaps more benefits than any other word.

Maybe you'd rather use another word for calling the dog. Some trainers believe the sound of HERE carries farther. A daughter of a friend has said she would never be caught pleading "Duke COME," – not in her neighborhood! Use whatever you like. Your pup doesn't care. He'll come to the word GO if you train him that way. A fellow I hunted with in Montana used words he made up, so nobody could easily steal his dog. If they did, the dog would seem useless because it didn't understand commands in English or any other language. For most amateur trainers, however, I think it's best to use whatever command words come most easily and naturally to your lips. You don't want to be groping for words when the situation calls for an instant command.

When the pup comes running, hold the bowl low, say HEEL as you stride forward, and little Buckshot will follow with his nose in the food. Another command is introduced.

Holding his food bowl, call "Buckshot, COME!" so he'll run to your side. If he's hesitant, squat down to his level to encourage a quicker response. Squatting seems to be a play invitation that puppies and even older dogs respond to almost automatically. Hold the bowl low enough for him to smell it. Still holding the bowl low, say "Buckshot, HEEL" and walk several yards. He'll usually follow eagerly, nose in the bowl or close to it. If you have a pup that loves to roam and explore more than he likes to eat, control him with a leash.

When you stop, place the bowl out of reach, and say WHOA as you restrain the dog. Make the restraint brief at first; it should only last a few seconds. Then, still restraining Buckshot, reach for the bowl, and *give the pup his food where he's standing at whoa.* Praise him with "Good WHOA!"

Why don't you release the pup instead of handing him the bowl? Because we want Buckshot to learn to stand patiently and contentedly, knowing that right there is where he gets the reward. Dogs learn from us, even when we don't know we're teaching. Sometimes it's so subtle we don't ever recognize it. In this case, if we released the pup to go to the food, he'd learn that WHOA means stand nervously and impatiently while looking for an opportunity to break. Obviously, that's not what we're trying to teach a bird dog. The WHOA command is needed to steady him on point. It should never urge him to break.

Before giving the pup his food, stop and restrain him, saying WHOA and placing the bowl out of reach.

To my knowledge, this is the first book to recognize the importance of teaching WHOA in this manner. It is common practice to teach a WHOA-COME sequence. The trainer conditions the dog to stand at WHOA while he walks around and away from the dog, finally stopping and commanding COME. It seems logical. Two commands are learned in one exercise. The dog is eager to be released from restraint, so the COME command gets added reinforcement.

You don't want Buckshot becoming anxious to break the WHOA command, so don't say OK and release him. Reach out and get the food after a few seconds of WHOA.

Buckshot is fed right where he stood at WHOA.

Obviously, because bird dogs have been trained in this or a similar manner for a long time it must work. So why try to change a long-standing tradition? Because the tradition produces too many failures, too many dogs that want to creep on birds, too many that want to break and flush. Yes, they can be pressured or shocked into eventually becoming steady on point, but the conflicting signals (be eager to break, but be steady) cause too many washouts, too many dogs that have screwed up heads, too many dogs that become flushers instead of pointers, and too many that end up as pets or destroyed.

If avoided for no other reason, sending the dog conflicting signals simply causes too much wasted training time to make sense. The intention of the Speed-Train system is to use methods that teach most efficiently and never cause problems that require extra time to correct.

Important: If you're very perceptive, you noticed that while training we said "Buckshot, COME." "Buckshot, HEEL." We didn't say, "Buckshot, WHOA!" We said WHOA without his name. There's a good reason. Dogs have a tendency to come toward you when their name is called. That's fine for COME and HEEL. But WHOA is a restraint command. In no way do we want to urge movement.

Equally important: Dogs are place learners and creatures of habit. At first, it can be very confusing to the dog if you move from place to place as you train. Do the food-bowl sequence in the same location until the puppy seems to be catching on, then move to a second location until he does well there, too. Then alternate locations. After that, add a third location. Dogs need to become accustomed to doing a thing in four to six different places before they thoroughly understand that the commands are to be obeyed everywhere.

Warning: One more reminder. This is puppy training, not serious obedience, and it works only if the puppy is motivated by rewards of food, fun, and praise. He will learn quickly, if you carry out the instructions calmly and persistently, because the system arranges for him to be a winner *every* time. He'll also gain great confidence in himself and you. If you lose your temper and yell, however, you'll consequently waste a great deal of time in overcoming the results of your mistakes.

Step 9

Running a Hunting Pattern

Running a hunting pattern is called quartering. It means your dog will race back and forth in front of you in windshield-wiper fashion. When actually hunting, the dog will not run such a formal pattern. He'll quickly learn to reach out and hunt objectives (for example, fence rows, weed patches, brush piles, and so on), where birds live. It's wise to teach your dog to quarter because it gives you a certain amount of control over range and area hunted. It's also wise to introduce quartering at this early age while the pup wants to go wherever you lead. Quartering is especially important for pheasant, grouse, and woodcock dogs.

This will be your pup's first introduction to a whistle. Get a double whistle; one end should sound like a police whistle, and the other mouthpiece, without a bead, should not trill and should be blown more softly. Do get a whistle. Some hunters pride themselves in having voices loud enough to reach the dog. Others find yelling offensive in the outdoors, not to mention that it spooks all the game within earshot. Too much whistling is offensive, too, but if kept to a minimum, which you will, it will sound too much like birds to spook the wildlife. Once you own a dog whistle, carry it in the outdoors even when no dogs are along. (Carry it especially when big-game hunting in strange territory. You and I have been "turned around" a time or two, of course, but others have become lost. Usually they burn up their ammunition firing three-shot distress signals long before anyone realizes they're lost. If you have a whistle, you can blow three short, three long, three short SOS signals forever. Even if you're injured or in a weakened condition, you can stick the whistle between your lips. Just breathing through it may make enough noise to alert a trained rescue dog.) The Scott Company makes an inexpensive plastic whistle. I like its tone. If you feel better dressed wearing a horn whistle, those are widely available from supply catalogs, too.

Little Buckshot, wanting nothing more at this point than to go along with you, will probably stand timidly by your side, waiting for you to move. Don't.

Boredom will soon teach what you can't. He'll leave your side to explore the world.

Take little Buckshot to a bare field, clipped pasture, or fairly large expanse of lawn. If the place is new to him, he may be timid about leaving your side. It's difficult to train him to venture forth, or range out, but there's no need. A little boredom will do that for you. Just stand there. He'll soon get sick of that and move out. The grass is short, if there is any, so there are no high weeds to inhibit the little fellow's movements. The space around him is open, so he can see there's nothing to fear. In fact, the openness will encourage him to range out in search of something interesting.

Watch for Buckshot to reach the limit of courage for his first excursion and look back for reassurance. Blow a rather soft, two-second-long whistle on the mouthpiece without the bead, raise your arm to point in a direction opposite to the one in which the pup ran, and simultaneously walk in that direction. Buckshot will automatically turn and follow. He has four legs, and is charged with youthful excitement, so he'll run right on past you. Great! Let him run until he looks around again. Then whistle, give the arm signal, and once again walk in the opposite direction.

If Buckshot happens to be bolder than expected, and runs farther than about 50 feet without turning back for a look, blow the whistle, anyway. It will get his attention, and he will look. Then signal, turn, and walk away so he'll follow.

When Buckshot looks back for reassurance, blow a long tone on your whistle, point your arm away from the pup, and walk in that direction.

Once you get your pup turning to the whistle, he'll run back and forth while you just do the body motions instead of walking.

Each time he races past, praise him with, "Good boy," or an excited, "Look at him go!" Your approval spurs great enthusiasm for the new game. Don't destroy the novelty. Turn the dog perhaps six times, then quit, and give Buckshot lots of pets for being such a marvelous pup. Repeat this exercise two or three times a week, if possible. Just don't make it boring by overdoing it.

This is the beginning of whistle control. Bird-dog pups seem to have a natural interest in birdlike sounds, a fact that makes most of them incredibly easy to train to the whistle. It's a game now, but later on you'll be able to turn Buckshot away from posted land or toward an area you believe holds birds. You'll also be able to turn him if he starts ranging farther to either side than you think he should.

Caution: Do not decide you'd rather use a short blast, or some other whistle sound, in place of the long note. If you give a short *toot,* and it isn't obeyed, especially later on, there's no choice but to punish. If you *toot* again, he'll soon learn that he doesn't have to respond the first time, or the second, or the third. When he's older, and at considerable range, catching him to administer punishment may be quite a job. On the other hand, the long tone usually can be continued until the dog does respond.

Step 10

Early Fun Fetch

Let's try little Buckshot on fetching. Field trials held from horseback have dominated bird-dog competition for most of this century, and they do not test retrieving. As a result, breeders have neglected to select their stock for the retrieving instinct, so most bird dogs don't have much of it.

If you bought one of the short-tailed or "versatile" breeds—such as a German shorthair, Weimaraner, pudelpointer, vizsla, wirehaired pointing griffon, drahthaar, and some Brittanys—you may have had a better chance of getting a dog with strong retrieving instincts. There are, unfortunately, no guarantees because as fast as a new breed is imported to America, someone decides to make them over in the image of the Americanized English pointer. Shorthairs have become much racier in build by outcrossing on pointers. You can see Brittanys with strangely short hair and the legs of a pointer while the head may look more like that of a Brittany. Some individuals have retained natural retrieving ability; some have not.

On the other hand, relatively new field trials, such as Shoot-to-Retrieve events, are intended to develop and enhance all of a hunting dog's instincts. Most of these dogs are pointers and setters that, in general, have excellent pointing instincts while their retrieving characteristics are on the comeback.

Tennis balls are excellent for starting pups on retrieving. They're action-packed. Toss a dummy, and it plops. Throw a tennis ball, and it will bounce against the wall, fly back off, and bounce two or three more times going across the lawn. A pup can scarcely ignore that. Dogs are genetically programmed to chase.

Tennis balls are full of bouncing action to get the attention of a young pup whose retrieving instincts may not be the greatest.

What happens when the pup catches the ball is another matter. Say COME, and Buckshot just may do it. Let him continue to hold it, if he wants, while you sing high praises about his amazing delivery. When you do take the ball, throw it again immediately. Say FETCH. Maybe he'll do it again. If he does it a third time, thank your lucky stars, praise the pup, and quit for the day. Try it again the day after tomorrow. Never push for fetch, after fetch, after fetch. Even lots of Labrador retrievers get bored with too much of a good thing. Most bird-dog pups get bored with retrieving in a big hurry.

If your pup chases the ball, then smells it and walks off disinterested, tie a string to the ball to keep it animated. To attach a string, tie the string's end very tightly on the shank of a large finishing nail, just below the head. Shove the nail through the center of the ball. When the sharp end is poking out, grip it with pliers, and pull. The relatively small head of a finishing nail should pull through the ball, bringing the string along. Knot the end of the string repeatedly until you have a cluster of knots that won't pull back through the ball. When you throw the ball now, you can keep it moving in little jerks until the pup does grab it.

What will he do? You're prepared with a check cord if the pup tries to run off with the ball.

You're lucky. He looks up toward you. He's coming, but the slack is out of the check cord, just in case.

Another likelihood is that the pup will grab the ball, but decide it's fool-hardy to give such a nice toy to you when he can run off and play with it. If there's a string on the ball, *do not play tug of war.* That's a good way to start hardmouthing. Instead, pull a diversionary tactic. Take off running, not at the dog, and not directly away, but somewhat perpendicular to the pup so the animation of you running across his line of vision will urge him to chase. When he catches up, reach down and grab him, laughing and petting and making big fun of it while you collect the ball, if it's still there, from his mouth. If he dropped it, go back and pick it up.

From now on, put a check cord on Buckshot's collar as well as a string on the ball. Animate the ball until he grabs it. Repeat FETCH, and urge him in gently with the check cord, offering praise as you take the ball.

Hold out your hand to accept the delivery, but say nothing.

If Buckshot is fetching a ball without a string on it, but one day decides he'd just as soon keep it, even after you've said COME, pull the same diversionary tactic. Do not repeat COME a second time. Never again use the COME command in conjunction with retrieving. This command is too valuable to risk losing by helping the pup discover that he really doesn't have to obey it if he doesn't want to. From now on, use a check cord on his collar, and let FETCH mean the whole exercise—find it and deliver it to me.

You have the ball. Now's the time for enthusiastic praise. Giving the praise as the dog comes could actually stop him because he might assume he already did whatever it was you wanted.

For a disinterested pup, it may help to smear a few drops of bottled pheasant or quail scent on the ball.

Swapping the ball for a tasty bit of meat upon delivery helps encourage the more gluttonous-type pups. Most bird-dog pups, however, are more excited by play than eating and may even avoid or resist the reward.

The rule of thumb with early fetch training is try it, but don't belabor it. If it works, nurture it. Keep it fun. If the pup isn't interested, drop the whole thing for now. Forcing it at this tender age can destroy the whole program. There's plenty of time to teach retrieving after the pup is grown and can stand the pressure.

If a pup has no interest in the ball, adding a string to jerk it and keep it "alive" will help. But here's what will happen if you don't keep the check cord on the dog's collar for control. It ends in a tug of war that leads to eventual hardmouth.

In the meantime, watch how that non-fetching pup behaves as he continues to grow. When he's free in the yard and alone, does he drag sticks, cardboard, rags, or whatever is loose, or will come loose, to a certain place where he pretends to "kill" and tear these things to shreds? If he's carrying objects, grin big; later force-fetch training will be much easier.

Step 11

Larry's Launcher

You've had Buckshot for a few days now. You've awakened his nose, and he uses it. He accepts a leash or short cord, so dragging a longer, lightweight check cord will be no big deal if we need to use it. For the pup's size, about 30 feet of one-quarter-inch woven cord will be just fine. If the light cord tends to tangle in your particular cover, you might have to switch to about 20 feet of stiffer, full woven three-eighth-inch cord.

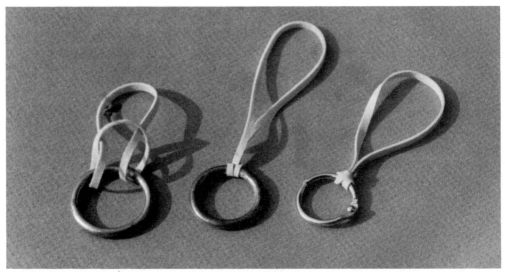

Seamless rings are best for my pole launcher, but split rings will do. Install rubber bands of appropriate sizes for the pigeons as shown here.

To install the ring and rubber band, hold the pigeon with its head in your palm and your thumb and first finger under its wings.

Buckshot has also been introduced to a running pattern. As a result of the nose awakening and food bowl training, he already responds to COME. It's too soon for him to really know HEEL or WHOA yet, but don't worry about it. He will. A more pressing need is Buckshot's introduction to birds. You bought a pup that points, right? Let's get him started!

Drop the rubber band over the wings with the ring to the rear and pull the rubber band over both wings.

When you are finished, the rubber band will be over the bird's back near the neck, under its wings, and once again, at the ring end, over the bird's back.

The first thing we need to do is plant the bird. You may know there are several ways to plant birds, including various bird launchers and methods of dizzying. They all work well in certain situations. When I first became aware of the importance of early puppy training, however, I realized that no planting methods were doing the job exactly right, so I searched for a new idea.

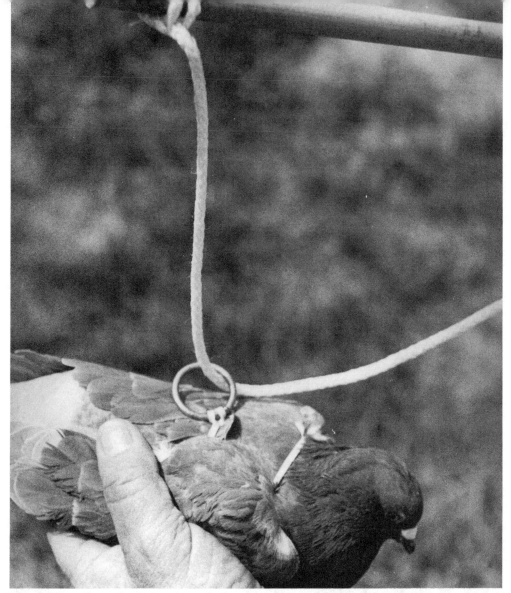

The cord on the pole slides through the ring. Tie the loose end to prevent the pigeon's premature escape.

I wanted the bird to be under my control, launched or flown when I'm ready, yet wide awake and free of other odors. I also wanted something inexpensive. If you can afford radio controlled launchers, fine. Use them. They're really great, but there are many great electronic devices for training. An amateur might find it hard to justify spending many hundreds, perhaps thousands, of dollars on equipment to train one dog. I was seeking a method anybody could afford.

If the pigeon is agitated and struggling, it will attract your pup's visual attention and he won't use his nose. Prevent that by tucking the bird's head under a wing.

Plant the pigeon in cover, being careful to lay it on the wing that its head is under. If necessary, use extra weeds or grass to prop the bird on its side so it can't easily roll over. Hold your hand on the bird until it seems quiet and willing to stay put. If you do this very gently, you will be gone before the bird gets up. Confused but unafraid, it will remain quietly out of sight in the cover as you approach with the pup.

The rubber band and ring idea popped into my head like someone dropped it on me. The best rings are seamless, but they're not readily available. Split rings will do. Slide the rubber band through the ring then back through itself, so the two are connected. Next hold the pigeon by the wings with your left hand. The pigeon's head is under your palm or perhaps the wrist, your middle finger is under the bird's right wing, your thumb is under the left wing, and your index finger is between the wings. Hook the rubber band under your index finger. Now pull the rubber band over both wings, bringing the ring to rest on the bird's back between the trailing edges of the wings.

At first, I ran a long string through the ring. When the dog pointed, I'd step on one end of the doubled string, jerk on the other to spook the bird into flight, then release the end from my hand when the bird was a foot or two off the ground. The free end of the string slid through the ring as the bird flew off.

Two things were still wrong. The strings were always tangling with something. The birds flew off low to the ground, too, teasing the dog into thinking he could catch them if he broke and chased.

When you are ready to launch, grasp the pole, unfasten the cord at the butt end of the pole, and raise the pigeon free of the cover.

I gave up on the idea for more than a year. Finally, one more new pup was needing a high, straight-up launch so he wouldn't try to chase. I fiddled with several ideas before it occurred to me to simply launch with a pole. I used several feet of stiff bamboo because I had it. The cord is tied to the end of the pole and slid through the pigeon's ring, after which it is tied to the pole's butt with a simple bow knot that's easily released by pulling on the free end. Light cord can be used with seamless rings. Heavier cord is necessary to prevent occasional catching if you use split rings.

Launch by "horsing" the bird upward as a boy might do a bullhead on a cane pole. Don't do it with such force that you break the rubber band.

Let go of the free end of the cord when the pole nears the vertical position, and the bird will be launched almost straight up.

The pigeon is planted in high grass or other cover where it can't be seen. It can move up and down the cord somewhat. The visible pole will help you guide the pup upwind toward the pigeon. Wrap a little fluorescent tape on the butt end if the pole is hard to see. When the pup points the pigeon, you will launch it by picking up the butt and freeing that end of the cord, but holding onto the cord as you swiftly raise the pole like landing a fish. When the pole is almost straight up, release the cord. The cord will slide through the ring as the bird climbs. Rings from 1 inch in diameter to 1¼ inches have worked well.

Matching rubber band size to pigeon size is important. Small, strong rubber bands on large pigeons can prevent flight by restricting the downward motion of the wings. Large or weak rubber bands on small pigeons will allow the birds to pull free and be gone, or at least off of the pole, when you arrive with the pup. Best sizes seem to be number 32 (3 inches long and ⅛ inch wide) for small pigeons such as "rollers," and number 34 (3½ x ⅛) for larger pigeons such as "homers."

Boxes of these rubber bands are reasonably priced at office supply stores. Department and discount stores usually have only mixed sizes. Always have several bands and rings made up in your pocket to replace those that may be lost or broken. Also, be sure to practice launching several birds before planting any for the pup. And practice launching the pigeons straight up so little Buckshot stands there, knowing he can't chase and catch them.

Step 12

Your Pup's First Bird

If you skipped everything else and jumped right back to bird work, as hunters are prone to do, go ahead and read this step. I know you will anyway. *But don't proceed with training without reading everything leading to this point.* You'll confuse your dog by not following directions.

This is your pup's big moment. Get it right. Rehearse the whole thing in your mind several times before you try it. You're going to expose your 8 to 12-week-old pup to the whole hunting experience in a capsule. Because the small pup is capable of absorbing so much behavior conditioning at this stage, and because none of his natural responses will be contrary to what's about to happen, we can Speed Train him into actually hunting before most dogs learn COME and WHOA. What he learns will establish good patterns for life.

Enlist a helper for these early experiences. Later, you can pretty well do everything yourself, but as you'll see, having a helper not only makes it easier for you, it will also teach your pup valuable extra information.

Choose the bird planting site carefully. You don't want a low depression where the wind might pass above the bird and fail to carry the scent to your pup. Nor should the site be so high that the wind carries the scent above the dog. Choose a fairly flat spot where at least a clump of cover will hide the pigeon from sight when you bring the pup into the wind toward the bird.

Do not come in directly against the wind. The pup would catch the distant faint scent which would gradually increase as he approached. That gradual increase could leave him in doubt as to when to point. To avoid that, you will come across the wind in the general direction of the pigeon, hoping to guide the pup to where he'll be 10 or 15 feet downwind of the bird when he suddenly catches the scent. If you chose a pup that points, and if you awakened his nose, the sudden, relatively strong bird scent will surprise him into a solid point.

After choosing the site, and knowing how you'll bring the pup in, plant the bird as described in step 11, but with one addition. Remember how you looped the ring on the rubber band? Form such a loop in the cord on your planting pole about two feet from the end of the pole. Place that loop around the neck of a freshly killed pigeon. You now have a live pigeon tethered on the cord by rubber band and ring, plus a dead bird tied higher in the cord.

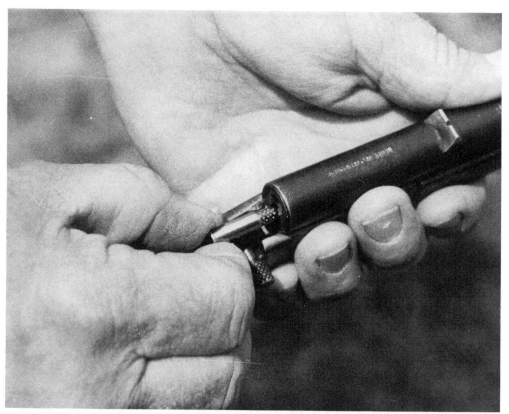

For Buckshot's first "hunting" experience, carry a rifle loaded with a .22 shotshell. You won't be killing anything, and the shotshell's mild report will scarcely be noticed.

Carry a rifle loaded with .22 caliber shotshells. You'd probably have trouble finding blanks, anyway, and nothing makes a softer, more easy-on-the-ears report than .22 shotshells. Do *not* use an ordinary cartridge. The crack may be too sharp. Forget, too, about a blank pistol, even if you own one. You don't hunt birds with pistols, and believe me, your pup will quickly learn to clue on what's going on when he sees you coming with a long gun. You want to build enthusiasm for the gun.

Blow a hawk whistle the moment the pup points. He will associate it with birds and eventually it will become your command to hunt close.

After Buckshot's point, have your helper launch the live pigeon. Shoot the .22 shotshell as your helper brings the pigeon pole back to earth with the dead bird that's looped in the cord. Buckshot associates the gun with the bird falling out of the sky and rushes forward to get the bird. Control his return with the check cord. He has had a complete hunting experience in capsule.

This is optional, but you might also carry a hawk whistle. It will be to your lips as the pup approaches the bird scent. The moment the pup points, blow the whistle as lightly as possible to get the hawk sound. Later, as the pup becomes accustomed to it, you can blow it loudly. If kept up, you'll get two things out of the whistle when hunting. Wild game birds are deathly afraid of hawks and will not flush prematurely if they believe one is near. By that time, your dog has also connected the hawk sound with bird scent. Blowing the whistle will draw the dog in to hunt an area where you believe there are birds. It becomes the command to hunt close. It continues to work as long as you don't overuse the whistle when no birds are present.

As you lead little Buckshot downwind of the pigeon, your helper will walk toward the bird, but have him hang back a bit so he doesn't get there before the pup points. He should be close, however.

Buckshot points! Now it's decision time. Do you want your pup to be steady-to-wing and maybe even shot, or are you like the vast majority of hunters who would just as soon stand at ready and have the dog do the flushing? If you want a steady dog, stay beside him and have your helper reach out, grab the pole, and launch the live bird. As he does, be ready to restrain the pup. It may pay to have a short cord on him. Fire the .22 shotshell as the bird flies.

If you'd rather have the dog flush the bird, your job is much easier. Allow your helper to grab the pole, then give a command – FLUSH, GET IT OUT, or whatever you like – and step toward the bird. Buckshot will undoubtedly break point and rush past you toward the pigeon. Your helper quickly launches the live pigeon, and you fire the .22 shotshell. If Buckshot breaks before your FLUSH command, say it the instant he starts moving. That makes his mistake all right. You won't foul things up with an angry correction, and Buckshot is still learning to connect the command with the action.

Buckshot may watch the live bird fly away, or he may see the dead one fall as your helper brings the pole back to the ground. If he sees the dead bird come down, he'll run toward it. Say FETCH the instant he starts. If he didn't see the dead pigeon, say FIND IT and walk toward the bird. When he finds it, say FETCH, and pick up the pole. When he grabs the bird, repeat FETCH, and gently draw the pole toward you so Buckshot won't have to drag the weight. If the pup needs urging to bring you the bird, use the check cord. Pulling on the pole would likely create a tug of war that would be the start of hardmouthing.

There's nothing as exciting as a bird to a well-bred bird dog, so there's no sense trying to swap a food reward for the pigeon. Just let him hold it a little longer while you lavishly hug and praise him.

You have just arranged for tiny Buckshot to go through all stages of a hunt. While it seems like a lot to remember, he will amaze you because it's all so natural to him.

If you can only train on weekends. give him his next bird tomorrow. After that, plant two, not more than three, pigeons each Saturday and Sunday that you can. If you're not restricted to weekends, let a day pass while he thinks about this experience and generates a longing to repeat it. Give him a couple of planted birds on the third day. After that, two or three birds twice a week is plenty. Too much of a good thing destroys the pup's anticipation and enthusiasm.

This was an alternative to the pigeon pole that we've tried with limited success. The dead pigeon was looped in the cord attached to the launcher's trigger mechanism.

One more thing. I didn't mention this earlier because you already had so many things to remember to do at the correct times. After that first bird, pay attention to how long Buckshot holds his points. Count the seconds he holds point before you command him to flush the birds. If he breaks to flush before the command, go ahead and give the command the instant he moves, but remember the number of seconds he held point.

The launch went fine, and there was no problem getting the dead bird down to the pup, but the noise of the launcher was disturbing to the pup. The greatest disadvantage, however, was the pigeon flying away across the ground, urging the pup to chase, a problem that does not occur with the pigeon pole.

If you notice that he broke in 10 seconds, next time wait only about five seconds, then command him to flush. If you want him to be steady-to-wing and shot eventually, have the helper simply flush the pigeon in five seconds. The idea is to be giving the command, or be flushing the bird, before he breaks. Once Buckshot seems as if he's waiting for the command, or waiting for the helper to flush, start making it six seconds. Gradually add one or two more seconds until you have him holding a minute or more before the flush.

Step 13

Introducing Water

A pup may take to water like a duck, or have a lifetime aversion for it. It all depends upon how you introduce it. The best way to kill water-love is to pick an overcast day during cold weather and insist that the pup learn to swim whether he likes it or not—while you stand comfortably on shore, of course. If he's bullheaded, throw him in. He'll hate water so much, he'll scarcely drink after that dip.

Bird hunting, however, sometimes occurs near water so retrieves from water are occasionally necessary. If the pup is of a versatile breed, and you intend to hunt ducks, it will be especially wise to make the right introduction to water.

Introduce water after a run on a hot day and make it shallow. After that first happy experience, a gradual change to deeper and deeper water presents no problems.

Age is not particularly important, except that usually the younger the pup, the more faith he has in you, and the more blindly he'll follow you into water. More important is the temperature. The water should be warm, and the day should be hot. Don't overdo exercise if the pup is very small, but walk him enough to get his tongue hanging and dripping. When you suddenly find a pond, and walk into the shallows, he'll be right behind, lapping liquid all the way. Walk out far enough for the water to wet his belly.

Buckshot follows me trustingly into the water.

In minutes, Buckshot is swimming short distances to chase the dummy.

That may be enough for his initial exposure, but watch his behavior. If he's very bold about it, get the pole and floating dummy you've brought along, and walk out to slightly deeper water. When Buckshot follows, float the dummy slowly past him to urge chase. If he's hesitant because of the water, give it up for today. If he chases (it will be a slow chase in water, of course) tease him into deeper water until he's swimming. The moment his feet start paddling, however, use the moving dummy to tease him back to where his feet touch bottom again. Do this two or three times, each time letting him swim a bit longer.

That's enough for today. No fear developed, so you can be pretty sure that Buckshot will freely enter water anytime you want.

If your pup is older than 4 months, it may not be quite as easy. Dogs hit a stage at about 4 months that compares with children's "terrible twos." The intensity of the stage varies greatly from dog to dog. Some very intelligent, cooperative dogs breeze right through it. The more willful, obstinate ones may suddenly go from the old "If you want to do it, so do I," to "No, I can't. It's impossible. It won't work. I'll die."

Don't force it. Just wait until after a rain, then run him until his tongue is about to drag on the ground. When he's begging mercy, find him a large puddle. He won't be afraid of that. If there are a few inches of water in a broad ditch somewhere, proceed to cross it repeatedly. He'll come along. Next time at the pond, he'll at least enter the shallows when he's hot. Before long you'll be able to coax him along into water deep enough for a short swim.

Step 14

Keeping It All Going

I know it's more fun to work Buckshot with birds but don't neglect everything else. Every time you have an especially tasty scrap from the table, do the FIND IT routine. Before long, Buckshot will "find it" so fast, you'll begin to wonder if he watched you drag the trail. Make the trail progressively longer, and put slight bends in it as your pup becomes more adept.

There's a definite limit on how long you can drag a trail with a piece of meat or skin before most of it is rubbed off on the grass or crumbled apart. In that case, you might switch to a rag or sock sprinkled with bottled pheasant or quail scent and dragged with a pole and string. A 50-foot and longer trail is now easy to make. He'll switch from meat scent to bird scent because by now he understands the command FIND IT and knows there is always a reward at the end. See that there is one, of course.

If he wanders off these longer trails at first, don't worry. Call him back, put your finger on the trail, and tell him FIND IT again. Later on, this practice will enable you to help keep him on a trail when you have seen where the bird ran.

It probably isn't wise to use a dead game bird as a drag. Some dogs start crowding and accidentally flushing their birds after that. Bottled scent, in my opinion, does not smell enough like the real thing to cause bumping, but using it helps your dog continue nose practice. If you're concerned about using it at all, then choose a scent the dog will never hunt — perhaps duck scent for a quail dog, or quail for a grouse dog.

Not all dogs, however, become good trailers. As a rule, the versatile breeds are better at this than are pointers and setters. It has nothing to do with quality of nose, but rather if the nose is carried high or low. If your high-headed English setter can't seem to get his nose down and trail, forget those long drags. Do continue the FIND IT practice with table scraps dragged short distances. He may dash about until he catches scent on the wind, then zero in on it instead of trailing, but he'll still be using his nose.

The smarter your pup is the sooner he'll figure out that the boss is dropping his own scent shower that is far easier to trail than that little bird-scented sock. OK, so he trails you to the treat. He's using his nose, and that's what a large part of this is about. I've used a fishing rod to cast the sock and reel it in to drag a trail with my scent absent but, by that time, the pup is usually too advanced for the distance I can cast. You might try it as an intermediate method between dragging the meat and dragging the scented sock. You can also not worry about it and be happy your pup is this smart.

As I said, you may lose interest in this when you start planting birds, but keep it up. You don't have to do it every day or even every other day, but if you aren't doing it at least once a week, you won't be able to capture your pup's mind before he's 4 months old.

Continue the food-bowl training on a daily basis. You have to feed him, anyway, and training takes just moments. If you're considering a self-feeder, forget it. People with self-feeders tend to get careless. Before long there are bird and rodent droppings in the feed. The dog's saliva falls into the food as he eats, and the chow at the bottom and corners of the tray soon molds. The first symptom of illness is often when the dog refuses to eat, and the fellow with a self-feeder may not know it for days. Besides the fact that the food bowl provides an opportunity for easy, quick, attention-getting training, I seriously doubt that anyone should own a dog if he's so disinterested in his dog that daily feeding is too much effort.

As Buckshot grows older and his legs become longer, he may also become too impatient to follow at heel with his nose in the bowl. He'll come when called because he's hungry, and he'll obey WHOA because you're restraining him, but unless you're controlling him with a leash, he'll soon race around instead of heeling. Don't worry about it, and don't think you've failed. Heeling is not all that important, and he has learned what the word means. There is plenty of time later to teach him that he must heel.

Keep up WHOA, however. Continue restraining him – gently and without anger or yelling – until he finally learns that he's supposed to stand and wait until he's given the bowl. When this occurs, begin counting the seconds he's content to stand. If it's perhaps 15 seconds until he tries to break, then start giving him the bowl at 10 seconds of WHOA for a few days. Then every couple of days add a second. Continue this until Buckshot is willing to stand a full minute before you hand him his food.

While you're keeping all of these other things going, you may be wondering what to do about Buckshot's irritating habit of jumping up on you. A quick knee in the chest is the quickest cure.

Keep up the NO, too. It's important for future control and to help avoid bad habits. If Buckshot is running totally free in the country, living in a fenced backyard, or staying in the house with you, use of NO will come automatically. The pup will provide you with ample opportunities to use it. With a kennel dog, you may have to contrive something while training or going for walks. When he tries to jump on you, perhaps. It should not be difficult to find something he shouldn't be doing.

Practice fetching, too, unless you find that Buckshot just doesn't have the instincts for it. If it's going to be a frustrating fight, forget it for now.

When you go for walks, give the whistle and hand signals to change direction fairly frequently. Don't make a pain of yourself over it, but use the signals enough that Buckshot is familiar with them and aware of his need to pay attention to your direction of travel.

If your pup is running free, the odds of him hunting close to you are much improved. Genes have a lot to do with the distance a dog ranges, but confinement is a sure way to make him run harder and farther to let off steam.

You're following the book, so your pup already comes when called, but here's a tip that will make you look like a brilliant dogman when your buddy's mutt won't obey the command. Simply get the dog's attention and scratch in the dirt. He'll have to come running to see what you have. You're deceiving the dog, however, so don't expect it to work very often before he begins ignoring this, too.

One thing to guard against is the possibility of Buckshot encountering game birds while running free. We want him to believe that birds are encountered only when he's with you, and then, only when you're carrying a gun. If he clues to these two things, and an intelligent pup will if given the chance, your worries about range are over. He'll be hunting for you. He might race far to the front in open country, but he'll shorten up again when more dense cover makes you difficult to see.

All pups can run free until about 4 months without developing self-hunting problems. Not all can continue to run free after that age, however. Some are natural roamers. They will gradually widen their territories, and will begin self-hunting something else if there are no birds. A confirmed self-hunter will also go self-hunting when you're with him. He'll accept *you* going along with him, if you can keep up, but *he* won't be going along with you. Keep an eye on Buckshot as he nears 4 months.

In fact, keep an eye on what the pup is doing while he is running free. If he's leaving the immediate area, he'll have to be confined in a yard or kennel. That's OK, too. You've achieved what you intended. He's bold, confident, knows how to get around, uses his nose, searches well, has enough sense to avoid danger, and best of all, he has developed a good working relationship with you.

Step 15

Pup Changes on Birds

In step 12 we had you loop a fresh-killed pigeon in the cord of the pole-type launcher. That works well when the pup is very small. You don't have to use a fresh-killed bird each time, either. Refrigerate it between sessions, then bring it out and let it warm a bit before each use.

If you're very, very fortunate, Buckshot will hold his points until told to flush. You'll succeed in increasing the length of his points by adding a second or two to each one before he's told to flush, or until the helper does it for you. If your fortune continues, he'll also fetch the dead birds every time.

More likely, Buckshot will discover that it's you who is blowing that hawk whistle. At first he thought it was the pigeon he was pointing, or another bird making the noise. It made him more cautious. He was less likely to try jumping in on the bird because he didn't know where it was or where they were. But he's catching on as he gets older. At this stage in a pup's life, 2 or 3 weeks is *much* older, and now he's wondering, "Why not try to catch that bird myself?"

He's learning other things, too. A bright pup may very soon learn that the quickest way to find the bird is to follow your scent trail through the weeds to where you planted the pigeon. That's not the way a dog should learn to hunt, so you have your helper go to the bird or even do the bird planting, while you make a roundabout circuit so Buckshot has no trail to follow. He has to use his nose to find the bird.

Eventually, the helper will have to be dismissed. With practice, it's not difficult to launch a bird with the pigeon pole and unsling the shotgun in time to make the kill. Note how well the pup stands and watches the straight-up launch instead of trying to chase.

Well . . . for a little while he must use his nose. But then he notices, sure enough, the helper is always right there where he finds the bird. He'll just speed things up by looking for the helper, and *then* he'll sniff out the bird in that vicinity. "If the boss wants Speed Training," Buckshot says, "we'll give him Speed Training."

Believe it or not, that's just what we get. I know you're thinking it's dumb to let the helper go to the bird in advance, but right now it's not. Young pups in these circumstances do benefit from learning that the bird may be near you, or that it may be near the helper. When Buckshot gets enough leg (approaching 4 months) you and a helper can walk down a field 50 yards apart, and that little fellow will probably do his level best to stay in front of you, and then the partner. Presto! You have already taught him to quarter in front of more than one person in the party. Some dogs never do learn that.

You can't keep on sending the helper to the pigeon, however. It will end with Buckshot on a check cord, pulling toward the helper the whole time. His searching would end. But if this is going to teach the pup to learn to hunt for both you and a partner, it will happen about as quickly as his mind connects the helper with the bird. As soon as you notice the pup going directly to the helper without hunting, begin having the helper go with you or come in after the pup is near the bird.

Buckshot will also outgrow interest in long-dead pigeons. It will become necessary to shoot birds for him. By that time, however, he should be accustomed to gunfire. When associated with birds flushing, the report of a .22 shot shell is scarcely noticed by an enthusiastic pup. After a few times, you can switch to .22 shorts, or even low-power long rifles, shot in a rifle, of course. The report is less sharp than in a pistol, but we also use a rifle because we want the pup aware that a long gun goes with hunting. Sometimes I cut the crimp off of shotgun shells and remove the lead to get weaker sounding blasts. And when I'm sure that high power .22's do not bother the pup, I carry both rifle (or shotgun) and a .22 pistol. (Shoot into the ground—unless it's rocky—when not using blanks, by the way.) When the pup points, I place the long gun on the ground and fire the louder sounding pistol on the flush. As with the rifle, begin with shorts in the pistol, then work up to high-powered long rifle .22's. If the pup accepts high powered .22's in a pistol, he's usually ready for the more booming blast of a .410, or even the weaker 20-gauge load. You can identify the weaker load by ⅞ oz. of shot being indicated on the box rather than a full 1 oz. of shot.

Advancing to louder gunfire goes rapidly for most pups because they're so enthusiastic about the bird that they give the firearm scant attention. If you notice a sensitivity to sounds of the gun, despite following the directions outlined here for systematic introduction, you could have a pup genetically inclined toward gun-shyness. There are two types of gun-shyness: genetic and manmade. The latter is caused by too many, too loud blasts coming too soon for the pup to become adjusted. Few amateurs will cure manmade gun-shyness with conventional methods, and genetic gun-shyness is many times more difficult to correct. If you have either form of gun-shyness cropping up, I'd recommend desensitizing the dog with a tape recording designed for this purpose. Such tapes are available from Master's Voice (see appendix).

The tape first soothes the dog with music, then introduces gunfire at an almost subliminal level along with the music. Gradually, over segment after segment, gunfire volume increases until it's as loud as the music. After that, music loudness is gradually diminished until at last it disappears and nothing is left but gunfire. If used as directed, it works well. I tested it and cured a third generation gun-shy dog that I had already failed to cure by conventional methods. If you have caused the gun-shyness, the tape can cure that, too.

Bird training will have to be postponed if you're dealing with any forms of gun-shyness. If you don't postpone bird work, you'll soon have a pup that is bird-shy as well as gun-shy. He'll become a "blinker," actually skirting around birds when he smells them because he knows that pointing a bird will result in the gunfire he fears.

If your pup tries to break point, use your check cord. Tie a loop in it about eight feet behind the dog. When he's on point, come up the check cord and shove a mushroom stake through the loop into the ground.

A more likely problem than gun-shyness will develop from Buckshot's intelligence and growing confidence in his own ability. He may decide not to wait for the shotgun to bring down the pigeon. Instead, he'll just break point before you arrive, and catch it himself.

He could do that with a planted pigeon, so watch for the slightest hint of this being in his mind. If he so much as makes a step toward the pigeon, make sure you have a check cord on him before you let him find the next one.

Don't become too overwrought about this. You see, the pup is figuring out that this is a game. He's tipped off by somebody's scent always being with the bird. He likes the game, but he's not above trying shortcuts. Just control him so he doesn't get the notion that bumping birds is permitted.

The next step is to use quail from a recall pen. These birds can be flushed out of the pen and hunted like wild quail. You don't plant them, so your scent isn't present when Buckshot points. They don't smell quite the same as wild birds because wild birds eat a different diet, but it's a vast improvement over planted birds. The main advantage is that when a pup tries to catch these birds, he can't. They'll fly whereas a planted pigeon usually can't. Eventually, these free-flying quail will teach an intelligent pup that if he is to ever get a bird in his mouth again, he'll have to stop chasing them. Of course, you *never* shoot a bird that he flushes without pointing, or even one that he points and flushes before told to do so.

Many of you, however, will want to continue with pigeons as long as possible. With pigeons, you don't need the big training area required by recall quail. If clumps of cover are arranged to hide the bird from sight (to make the pup use his nose) pigeons can be used nearly anywhere, even in the backyard.

With the check cord securely staked, you can circle the dog and go to the bird.

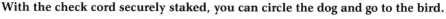

Make the flush and shoot the bird while the tethered pup watches, then release him for the retrieve.

To control the pup, use the check cord and a tie-out stake with a mushroom head. Tie a loop in the check cord about six feet behind the snap. If the earth is soft, you can come up from behind when Buckshot points, holding the check cord, if necessary, and shove the stake through the loop and into the ground. If the pup tries to creep forward, he finds himself restrained. Shoot the bird, or make a shotlike sound, then release Buckshot for the fetch, if there is one.

If the earth is hard, you'll have to drive the mushroom stake into the ground in advance. When Buckshot points, simply throw the check cord around the stake, and hold onto the loose end.

You'll have to modify the system when the stakes can't be shoved into earth that is too dry and hard. Using a hammer or maul, drive the stakes downwind from the bird, so they'll already be in place when Buckshot points. Simply slide the check cord's loop over the mushroom head. It may become necessary to quickly tie a new loop if the pup goes on point not quite where you expected, but that's not a problem. Just ensure that the stake is always far enough from the pigeon that the free end of the check cord will never be long enough for Buckshot to reach the bird.

If the pup begins to fight the cord excessively as you move past him to launch the pigeon, try walking in a wider arc around him. It will seem less of an infringement on "his" point. The motions of stepping right past him can be an invitation to break.

Some pups will bounce around on the end of the cord no matter how you handle the flush. You do not want this to become a habit. In this case, it may be a good idea to switch to a launcher that you can trigger from a distance. It's an even more phony set-up than our pole launcher, though; not only is your scent involved, but now you also have the odor of the launcher. In addition, it stands to reason that anything made to contain a bird will also somewhat restrict the flow of air and scent from the bird. I've resolved most of both problems – seemingly to the satisfaction of my dogs – by keeping the launchers in the pigeon loft where very soon they, too, begin to smell like pigeons.

Leon's launcher can be made or bought. The door is open here to show how to install the bird. The launcher is triggered by pulling the pin off of the bolt and out of the ends of the coiled spring.

When the halves spring apart, the hinged edges throw the bird into the air. Leon's launchers accommodate one pigeon or two quail.

Caution: If the springs become weak, or if the vegetation cushions the spring-open action, the bird may not be launched effectively.

A very economical launcher that hides easily in the cover and prevents Buckshot from getting his mouth on the pigeon, even when something goes wrong, is the contraption devised by Texas quail hunter Leon Measures. It is made of plastic plumbing pipe and screendoor springs. You can put one of these launchers together yourself from Leon's plans, or purchase one ready to go. (See appendix for mailing address.)

When Leon's Launchers are working properly, they put the birds in the air. You see, the hinged part of the two halves of pipe rests on the ground. When the halves spring apart, their round surfaces lift the hinged edges up directly against the pigeon's breast. This action not only throws the bird upward, it also startles the bird into sustained flight, so the birds aren't simply dumped on the ground.

I do have some cautions. Don't store these launchers in the closed, or "set," position because this weakens the springs. The launchers will not open with the proper snap, and birds will be just dumped out on the ground. Fix weak springs by shortening or replacing them. Also understand that this device was invented in a part of Texas where 20 quail would be happy to share 10 blades of grass as a hiding spot – if they can find that many. When I tried the launchers in Illinois' wheat stubble, or high grass, it tossed the birds poorly. The vegetation was cushioning the spring-open action. Clear away enough cover so the launcher rests right on the ground.

You also may want to spray these launchers with camouflage paint. The pipe's light color is too easily seen through vegetation. It encourages sight pointing as well as trying to jump in on the birds because the dog knows right where they are. Paint is a foreign stink in the field, of course, so weather the launcher for a few days, wash it off when the paint is thoroughly dry, then keep it in the pigeon loft a few more days before using it. Stick your nose in it. If you can smell it up close, you dog will smell it from at least 50 feet away.

The pin of this bird grenade is attached to a string which you pull to launch the pigeon. When the action starts, you will forget that the string was ever in your hand. I've found strings and pins 20 and 30 feet away. Some perhaps tangled in my feet or the dog's, left the area entirely, and were never found. It's a waste of time to search for it, and it's annoying to make a new pin, so attach a second, but short, string from the pin to the launcher frame. Now the pin and string won't be lost.

As suggested earlier, the advantages of Leon's launcher are:

1. You can flush the bird from a position behind the dog, thus reducing Buckshot's urge to jump in as you walk past.

2. If something goes wrong, and the pup decides to jump in on the bird without additional urging, all he gets is a mouthful of plastic. If this occurs, pick him up, return him to the site of his point, and stake him by the loop in the check cord—all without a word, or growl, or even a sigh out of you. He needs to know that his behavior is unacceptable, but at less than 4 months old he is not psychologically capable of dealing with, or even knowing about, the angry explosion developing inside you. He is giving—and must continue to give, if puppy training is to work—his full, unfearing trust.

Step 16

Little Puppyhood Ends

As little Buckshot approaches 4 months, or thereabouts, the period of almost total willingness to follow in your footsteps is coming to a close. Somewhere around 4 months, our ingratiating little pup begins to have a mind of his own.

It's an awkward stage for further training. That incredibly receptive stage is finished, yet the pup is still too psychologically immature to withstand the pressures of severe training. It's a no-win situation. If you continue training, he will often test your authority. If you prove your authority at this time, you'll rasp the edge right off of his enthusiasm, and he will never become the superb hunting companion he might have been.

It's wiser to call the puppy training finished. Continue to let Buckshot follow trails to table goodies occasionally, but not as often as before. Once every week or two is plenty.

The food bowl is still a good tool to keep reinforcing the COME command, but most dogs at this age no longer HEEL beside the chow in your hand. Making the pup continue to earn his food by obeying WHOA is still an excellent idea, however.

The pup will probably continue to point sparrows and the like, but as soon as he starts trying to do things his own way on planted pigeons, cease training. You can continue using strong flying quail from a recall pen, if you like, but even that's not necessary. Buckshot's instincts have been awakened. He firmly believes there is nothing so much fun as hunting birds with you, and unless you teach him otherwise, that notion is set for life.

When Buckshot's willingness to follow in your footsteps ends, he might also decide he'd rather keep the bird than deliver it. Prepare for this by turning your left side to the dog to accept the bird.

If he hesitates in finishing the retrieve, you're already in a position to move away from him.

Running away will urge him to follow.

When he catches up with you, accept the bird in exchange for profuse praise.

I prefer to let the pup continue to run loose quite a lot as long as he stays out of trouble. I also like to interact with him so he continues to grow better mentally than he would alone and in the kennel. That's about all, though, for several months.

If he was born this year, I like to give him his first hunting season without formal obedience training. He should be hunted alone. I'll put up with some pretty sloppy stuff that first season just to reinforce his love of hunting. I don't start serious obedience training until the pup is emotionally mature enough to accept it, which is usually when he's about a year old.

Considerable space has been devoted to puppy training because only you can do it, because this very early training is poorly understood, because no training you do is more important, and because never again in your dog's life will you get so much return for so little time. While its been given lots of pages, much of it has been spent in explaining why. Comparatively little actual training time is used, and the whole program only lasts for about 2 months.

I hope you didn't goof off those two months. There's no going back. Frankly, my friend, if you did these few simple things for about 8 weeks, your dog probably received more training than most dogs *ever* get. Some of you who did this early training will be so surprised and satisfied by your dog's first season, that you won't feel the need for further training. He won't be a finished bird dog by any means, but who's to argue if you're happy and content with how he hunts!

Part 2

The Adult Dog

Step 1

Outsmarting the Yearling

Young dogs go through three phases that seem intended to initiate human insanity. The first comes at about 4 months. We stopped the little puppy training at that age, so we missed most of that grief. Fortunately, it was over by hunting season in our spring-born pups, so we avoided it then, too. Even so, willfulness at 4 months is not all that hard to deal with. The worst stage comes at around 2 years old—but forget that for the moment. What we have to deal with now is stage two, and that one is difficult to circumvent.

Depending upon who claims to be the authority, you will hear that stage two occurs at 8 months, 8 to 12 months, 10 to 12 months, or 11 to 14 months. That's a major spread considering the general agreement on 4 months for stage one, and 2 years (give or take a month or two), for stage three. At first, I wondered who was wrong. The more I paid attention, though, the more I came to believe that they're all correct. I suspect that the reason for this age range springs from widely varying rates of maturity. Within the breeds, females usually mature faster than males, but the rate of maturity may vary even more between breeds.

Whatever the sex or breed, though, the pup that was so willing and agreeable up to four months, and that perhaps even hunted reasonably well during its first season, will now begin to contest your leadership. Even the intelligently submissive dogs conclude they know how to do it better. The dominant dogs, and some of those that are the less intelligent, become downright obnoxious about it.

There's no way to avoid this one. Your pup is approaching a year of age, and he's now mature enough for serious training. Up until now, we've made it pleasant and rewarding for the little fellow to develop his instincts and learn what his job will be. At this point, however, the fun of doing things his way is becoming vastly more rewarding than our tidbits and praise. It's time for a new dimension. The operative word is "must." He *must* learn what he *must* do. We're no longer suggesting a course of action and rewarding the pup when he does it. We're showing him a course of action that he must follow, or he makes things very uncomfortable for himself. Let's say that again. It's extremely important. "*He* makes things uncomfortable for *himself.*"

Why not "*we* make it uncomfortable for him?" Ask yourself, what does a dog learn when *he* does something wrong and *you* whip his butt? He learns that you don't want him to do that. He'll think twice about doing it again when you're around, but sooner or later he'll try it anyway. About the third time he's whipped, he'll stop doing that thing when you're around, but he still *wants* to do it. And eventually he will. You haven't really cured him of anything.

On the other hand, suppose as the dog trots past, you order WHOA. He doesn't stop as you've ordered, so something grabs him by the neck and flips him tail over toenails. He suspects you because he didn't obey the order. You're too far away, though. You're not even making eye contact, which he thinks you'd be doing if you were malevolently involved.

Later on, you'll be doing this with Buckshot on the ground cable. You'll be guilty as heck, too, because you arranged it. But he won't know it. Therefore, by not associating you with the punishing discomfort, he will not learn to fear or mistrust you.

On the contrary, you were the all-knowing benefactor trying to help him avoid that mistake. Didn't you see it coming and tell him WHOA to avoid it? He just didn't listen, *so he caused himself trouble.*

This series is an example of how to arrange things so Buckshot can conclude that he gets himself into trouble by not listening to you. Velcro anklets with **D**-rings are already on three of the dog's "ankles." Come up the check cord with a set of hobble connectors in hand. (See Scott catalog.)

Snap the connectors to the three anklets.

As you walk past Buckshot and pick up the pigeon pole, command WHOA.

Buckshot ignores your good advice, tries to catch the bird, and falls all over himself. He knows he did it to himself by ignoring your suggestion that he stand steady at WHOA.

See the difference? If we can arrange things so the pup thinks he did it to himself, he'll not only stop doing it—he won't want to do it anymore. The cure is quick. Best of all, when he decides he doesn't want to do it, the cure is usually permanent.

Some of you may be doubting this. Throughout little puppy training, I've insisted that you restrain your temper. Now the pup is old enough to take pressure, and I'm still saying don't be abusive. It seems unnatural to you. Your automatic response to the dog testing your authority is to lash out.

Trust me. I have great fondness for dogs, but they don't make a fool of me, and they shouldn't make a fool out of you. The world is not a painless place for man or beast, and I believe in swift punishment with a severity commensurate with the offense.

When possible, however, and it usually is, if I'm thinking, I want to administer whatever pressure or punishment the dog needs without his associating it directly with me. Substituting thought for temper is not always easy, but the benefits in saved training time are enormous, and Speed Training, is, after all, the purpose of this book. The end results are a trusting dog and a bold, devoted hunting companion instead of a cowering boot polisher or a disobedient dog.

Step 2

If You Missed the Puppy Period

Some of you let that crucial 8 to 16-week-long puppy period slip by without getting the job done. Maybe you even tried those training techniques after the period was over, and found they didn't work on older pups. Well, the pup didn't get trained, but you learned something: Either stick with your dog's timetable or get left at the station.

Other would-be trainers missed those crucial weeks because they didn't have this book, and a few of you didn't acquire the dog until it was too old for that period of easy training. Whatever the reason, you're all in the same boat, and rowing is harder than it might have been had you started earlier. You're about to learn what a professional trainer is up against.

All in one package, you have a dog with many, most, or all of these deterrents to training:

1. He is in his first seriously rebellious stage.
2. He hasn't learned to learn because he vegetated in the kennel for a year.
3. His nose hasn't been awakened to any better use than smelling other dogs' rear ends.
4. He has formed shy kennel habits.
5. If he has any bird interest at all, it's in sparrows because that's all he has seen.
6. If he points, it's sight pointing because that's the only way butterflies and sparrows can be pointed from inside the kennel.

If you've missed the little puppy period, it's doubtful that your dog will be interested in fetching a ball. You may have to use a dead pigeon or quail for more incentive. A cord on the bird will allow you to spin it and sling it farther.

If you're the fellow who acquired an older dog, I know what you're about to say: "But the guy told me this dog hadn't been fooled with, so it's unspoiled." So much for one more true-sounding lie. Worse yet, maybe you "rescued" this dog from the shelter. You're about to find out why the dog was there in the first place. He could be gun-shy, have no nose, won't hunt, or blinks birds. Like anything, few good dogs are free, and almost nobody pays money to a shelter to take a good dog off their hands. *Reconsider.* An amateur needs a dog with superior instincts, not a mutt that the pros wouldn't even touch.

Buckshot is also on a cord to insure his return.

I'd much rather suggest that you read all of part 1, then go buy the right pup, and start over. But I know you won't, so we'll try to get past this awkward situation and get on with Speed Training. You'll spend more time than necessary correcting faults and compensating for what wasn't done earlier, and the dog never will be as good as it might have been—the dog may even be a washout—but the choice is yours. Good luck.

Your first dilemma is the no-win situation faced by all pros. This yearling needs to have his bird interest sparked or improved. Allowing him to chase birds will do that. Some dogs eventually discover that they'll never catch birds, so they begin pointing, after which they can be trained without great difficulty. Less intelligent dogs simply make a habit of chasing, and that's hard to break later, so this method produces lots of washouts.

Maybe you can arrange a bare room with nothing in it but your young dog and a pigeon. If the pigeon can't find any place to land except the floor, eventually the dog will become interested and chase, until he catches the bird. A couple such birds might awaken the dog's interest, and chasing won't be as deeply ingrained. Of course, he'll learn that it's possible to catch a bird, and that may encourage him to break or creep while on point.

After a few successful retrieves to get the bird's odor, try hiding the bird in the grass and urging your young dog to find it in order to awaken his nose. Lead him to the vicinity on check cord, if necessary. Do not lay a drag trail with a game bird, however, because this causes some dogs to trail and flush live birds.

Perhaps it would be better to teach obedience first. Then you'd have control if the dog tries to creep or chase. Of course, obedience subdues a dog that hasn't first experienced the fun of hunting. Instead of hunting confidently, he looks to you for guidance. Unless you're a very good trainer, obedience before birds could make a plodding, half-hearted worker out of what might have been a flashy performer.

Rather let him chase? I forgot to tell you. Chasing generally widens a dog's range, and most hunters don't care for wide-running dogs. Among other things, they're harder to keep in close to hunt singles after the covey has been flushed and scattered.

Some of the puppy training can be useful even if you've missed that period. Your young dog probably won't follow the food bowl around, but Buckshot may HEEL behind the odor of baked liver or a piece of hot dog.

Treats can be used to introduce whistle signals, too. Obviously, these treats can't be continued very long in training, but they do speed understanding of the commands.

The best option may yet be starting with a new pup. Still not ready? OK. More of these older dogs will be given away as pets, or taken to the shelter, than would have been the case had their owners started them as pups, but we'll have to find a compromise method to begin their training. My personal choice is the Silent-WHOA system practiced by trainer Bruce Ludwig.

Step 3

The Silent-Whoa System

Professional trainers get everybody's mistakes, and Bruce Ludwig of Prescott, Arizona had a couple of dogs that were ignoring the spoken word. Their owners had chattered when attempting to train, so the dog tuned them out. Dogs can easily learn a few words, but strings of words are meaningless. WHOA, for example, can be grasped quickly. But if it's included in, "Now, dammit, Jake, I've told you this one hundred times; either WHOA, or I'll stomp your butt," the dog doesn't listen through all that mess long enough to catch a word he knows.

Sometimes, even when a dog has already learned a single-word command, he'll ignore it when it's buried in a string of words. A pro can have a dog whoaing beautifully, yet pretty soon the owner is back claiming the trainer sure messed up on that one. "Show me," the trainer says, and the owner says, "WHOA, Jake, you dimwit, or I'll break all of your legs." The dog knew WHOA, but the extra words meant to him that the WHOA command was terminated. He doesn't understand the other words, but he knows they don't mean WHOA, so he proceeds to do whatever he wants. He has done this so many times—start to WHOA, then quit—that he may even believe he is dutifully following a command that says, "Stop an instant, then do what you want."

Bruce Ludwig realized he'd have to retrain these dogs to stop, or WHOA, without the voice command. He started walking one of them on a short check cord. When the dog wasn't excited and straining at the collar, Bruce gave the rope a little flip that slapped it lightly on the dog's withers (on top of the shoulders, behind the base of the neck). Immediately after the light slap, Bruce snugged the rope to prevent forward movement. After a moment and before the dog even thought of trying to squirm free, Bruce walked forward, and the dog moved on.

Bruce Ludwig teaches Silent-WHOA by stopping the dog with a light slap of the cord or leash across the shoulders.

It takes lots of starts and stops, but the momentary pause doesn't last long enough to make the dog fidgety. This pause can gradually be lengthened by a couple of seconds at each stop until the dog is essentially standing at WHOA. The dog still isn't fidgety because he knows it doesn't last forever.

This is not just a marvelous technique for those owners who have chattering problems. A dog clues in on the tone of your voice as well. If you've been arguing with your wife, or if you just smacked your thumb with a hammer while fixing the kennel door, the dog can't help but catch your mood in the WHOA command. If you're on edge, so is he. If you sound ready to lash out, he knows he will be on the receiving end. He's nervous, and his concentration comes apart. Everything starts going wrong, and you think it's another "one of those days." It needn't be if you use the Silent-WHOA system.

Preventing the dog from picking up on your moods is the reason I like this method for those of you who are starting with older dogs. You already have enough problems to overcome without making more by becoming annoyed. This system is optional for those who started their pups at 8 or 9 weeks old.

If the dog lives in a kennel, I strongly suggest beginning this training inside a bare room, garage, or barn where visual distractions are minimal. Kenneled dogs, hoping for a romp, become terribly excited at the prospect of getting out, so they're hard to walk calmly without fighting the cord. They settle down much more quickly inside. When they do, walk them slowly and begin the lessons. After the dog is responding inside, continue the lessons outside, gradually lengthening the time at Silent-WHOA.

When the dog learns to stop without a vocal command, he's taught in the same way to stand steady for birds.

When the dog is holding his Silent-WHOAS in the field, Bruce leads him toward a planted pigeon, pausing along the way a few times to practice WHOAS. "I hope for a natural stop and point when he smells the bird," Bruce says. "If I get it, then I can shoot birds for the dog occasionally, and even let him fetch as a reward."

The dog also gets a snap of the check cord to reinforce the point and to condition the dog to understand that bird scent means WHOA, too.

"The dog that's not birdy, and doesn't point his birds, will have to be allowed to chase some pigeons to develop his interest," Bruce points out. "But that dog will never be what you hoped for."

After the dog is chasing, try him on a planted bird again. If he's interested, resume the Silent-WHOA training. If not, go back to chasing pigeons.

Once the dog understands that both the snap of the cord and bird scent mean WHOA, then add the vocal command. Snap the cord, and say WHOA. After a few times, switch it around. Say WHOA, then snap the rope. He'll soon realize that when you order WHOA, the silent command will follow. He starts anticipating it and stops on the vocal command. After sufficient practice, you will have the vocal command to reinforce the point, and perhaps stop creeping, when the dog is no longer on the check cord.

As we said, more late-starting dogs will wash out under this system than might have had they been trained as pups. The Silent-WHOA system is, however, easier on these dogs, and gives them a better chance than do conventional methods.

Those who started their dogs as pups needn't teach silent WHOA if those dogs are already holding their points well. If there is a tendency to creep, it would be wise to teach it so the dog becomes conditioned to the idea that bird scent emphatically means WHOA.

Extra observation: Maybe you haven't thought of it before, but this step is a good example of a dog's ability to understand more than one signal for the same command. The snap of the cord, bird scent, and the word WHOA all mean stop and stay right there. It has often been said that understanding three ways to give a simple command is the limit of a dog's ability. I don't know of a test that has established true limits, but three is *not* the limit. Some bird dogs learn to stop to bird scent, vocal WHOA, gunfire, and the flush of birds. I'll bet we can add snap of the leash to that list, too.

Step 4

Instant Whoa

I walked outside to feed my birds while deep in thought one morning. I had been teaching my dogs WHOA on a bench because being off of the ground makes them feel unstable. They're then less confident and bold, so they pay more attention and learn more quickly. What if they *really* had unstable footing, though? Wouldn't that be a super Speed-Train method of teaching WHOA? What could I use?

Suddenly, I was looking straight at an old, rusty, 55-gallon steel drum. "That's it," I thought. "The rusty surface is just rough enough for a dog to grip if he stands motionless. (A piece of canvas or other heavy cloth glued to a painted drum gets the same results.) If the drum were placed on the lawn, the grass would keep it from rolling as it might on a hard surface such as concrete, but any movement by the dog would make it roll on the grass nevertheless."

Perfect! I couldn't wait to try the idea. To make the lesson even more quickly understandable to the dog, I also threw a check cord over the limb of a tree. With the cord snapped to his collar, I could steady him somewhat by holding onto the other end of the rope. Obviously, I used his ordinary collar, not a choke chain—I didn't want to hang him. If he moved, though, so would the drum, and he'd slide off. Dogs have strong necks, so there was no fear of injury when using a regular collar. He'd be hanging there scrambling to get back onto the drum only for the few seconds it would take me to get there to help.

A rusty steel drum on grass provides exactly the right amount of instability to teach a dog WHOA almost instantly.

I lifted my dog to the drum slowly and gently, positioning his feet so he'd be balanced, then snapped the cord to his collar. "WHOA," I said, and stepped back, hand up in traffic-cop fashion, and holding the loose end of the check cord taut enough to keep the dog's head high.

With most dogs, on the first to third try you can back away and circle as widely as the check cord will allow.

The first young dog I tried training in this manner didn't move a muscle. I walked back and forth, hand still up, and saying WHOA occasionally while he stood like an ice statue—so still only his eyes showed animation. After a few moments, I lifted him off with great praise. He hadn't fallen off once! I had an instant training method for WHOA that would only need repetition to keep him from forgetting the lesson learned.

An extra bonus is the fact that you can immediately move to the front without the dog breaking. This conditioning is extremely valuable later when the dog is on birds, a time when a conventionally trained dog often tries to break when the trainer passes him to flush the bird.

That dog didn't slide off of the drum until some lessons later when I began circling him. I hid behind a tree trunk and, when he couldn't see me in his peripheral vision, he turned his head to look and lost his balance. I quickly put him back on the drum, stayed to the front, then finished the lesson. I don't think that dog slid off more than three times throughout the whole WHOA training.

Think of it! None of that constant neck jerking and pinching with a choke chain that you must do with ordinary WHOA training. It may *look* worse when the dog slides off, but he does it only a few times, and the regular collar won't even pinch his neck.

Intelligently submissive dogs rarely fall off the drum. Less intelligent and dominant types have more trouble. It's uncomfortable, but don't worry. He won't die, although he doesn't know that.

He can't scramble back on an unstable drum, so you'll have to help. Do it reasonably soon, but don't rush to the rescue. Let him believe he almost died.

I experimented with five dogs before deciding I really had a worthwhile idea. Three dogs were submissive, and two of those were intelligently submissive. Those two learned WHOA the first time on the drum. The less intelligent submissive dog took only three lessons before I could circle him without him falling. An intelligent dominant female had more trouble and tried to find a way out. Jumping off didn't work, and because the discomfort was self-inflicted, she didn't try again. Then she wanted to sit. As usual, the dominant dogs were slower learners because they always preferred to try their own ideas until proven wrong. The fifth dog, a rather stupid dominant male, gave me the most trouble on the drum. He would avoid eye contact, hoping I'd think he hadn't heard the command. Sure enough, though, he might have been hearing but he wasn't *listening.* He jumped off a number of times and also fell off easily when distracted. When I placed him on the drum, he'd try to lean on me to avoid having to balance himself. The rate at which he learned WHOA on the drum, however, was absolutely amazing compared to his rate of learning anything else.

The next step is to circle widely and hide for increasing lengths of times. Some dogs think they can break when you're "gone," but the more intelligent ones don't even try.

Even flying paper plates will not distract most dogs whoaed on the drum. It's incredible how fast they learn.

The sequence I worked out was a short introduction to the drum followed by every-other-day lessons which grew longer by a few seconds each time. When the dogs learned to stay balanced while I walked around, I'd circle as wide as my 50-foot-long check cord would permit. By then, they weren't even sliding off, so I added the distraction of flying paper plates. When they still remained steady, it was time to try WHOA on the ground.

The dog probably won't think WHOA applies off the drum, so leave the cord attached. When you give the hand signal for WHOA, keep the cord in your left hand, providing the familiar upward pull associated with WHOA on the drum.

I'll remind you that dogs are place learners. If you teach a dog to lie down on the patio, then say DOWN out in the driveway, that dog will probably be confused because the patio is missing. The place can be as much a part of the command as the word. As I said before, dogs may have to learn a lesson at four to six different sites before they know that the command applies everywhere. This is also true when WHOA is taught on a table or drum. As soon as their feet touch ground, they don't feel the need to obey the command.

Expecting that, my next step was to lift the dog to the ground beside the drum, leaving the check cord over the limb and still snapped to the dog's collar. The loose end of the cord was in my left hand. As I put the dog on the ground, I put my right hand before his face, traffic-cop fashion, and I said WHOA. As predicted, he saw no need to WHOA in the new circumstance and tried to take off. The instant he lunged, I pulled the check cord, his front end lifted off the ground, and the dog came to a halt. After a time or two, the dog heeded WHOA, and I could circle him at will.

With the upward pull of the cord still in effect, you can soon back away and circle the dog as if he were on the drum.

One very important aspect of this transfer of command-location is giving an upward pull on the check cord. That's the same direction of pull the dog felt while on the barrel. Two variables—the vocal WHOA and the upward pull— were the same while only the location of the dog's feet was different. Having two clues out of three greatly speeds the dog's acceptance of a new place, as compared to something such as the DOWN command mentioned earlier where only the voice command was the same.

What about a dog that tries to sit on the drum? You'll recall that a bitch of mine tried that trick. I snapped the check cord around her flanks, so she couldn't sit. If she fought it, she fell off the drum, nose down. She did once or twice, too, before learning the command. This is worth remembering because some dogs have a natural inclination to sit when ordered WHOA.

Important: Practice WHOA on and beside the drum two or three times a week. It takes weeks of repetition to deeply ingrain a restrictive command in a dog's mind.

Suggestion: Those of you who don't have a tree limb over which to throw the check cord aren't faced with an insurmountable problem. Maybe there's a play gym in the backyard. Temporarily fasten the swing seats and chains out of the way, and throw the check cord over the framework. Failing that, it's not difficult to make a wooden sawhorse the size of a swing-set frame. Brace it well so it's rigid.

As on the drum, fly paper plates to tempt the dog into breaking WHOA. If he does, correct it with a sharp pull on the check cord.

Want to make a dog rock solid on WHOA? After he has had some practice on the drum, place a piece of baked liver, or other goody, on his nose while at WHOA. Make him hold it a few seconds before putting it in his mouth. Add a couple of seconds each time after that. When he learns that WHOA pays big dividends, you have an apt pupil.

Bonus: Most WHOA training begins from behind or beside the dog. When the trainer steps forward, the dog wants to follow, and continues to want to follow, even after long practice. This can be a serious problem when you want the dog steady, and you move forward to flush birds. Many dogs must be circled widely so they won't break. During WHOA training on the drum, however, you are positioned in front of the dog and, after a few sessions, the dog does not want to follow you. He becomes thoroughly accustomed to you being in front so when hunting or training later on he won't be nearly as tempted to break and race you to the bird.

Step 5

Check-Cord Quartering

Those owners who did the puppy training may not need to teach quartering on a check cord. If the dog is turning to the whistle and hunting a reasonable pattern, that's all that's necessary.

For older unstarted dogs, however, the quickest way to teach quartering is on the check cord. Even pups older than 12 to 16 weeks are best started on the check cord. They no longer have that little puppy desire to stay close to you, so they reach out to explore. Without the cord, they quickly learn that it's only necessary to turn to the whistle when they feel like it.

Some trainers use cords as short as 15 feet. I prefer a 50-foot cord because I think it gives the dog more room in which to move and, therefore, the lesson is a better correlation with an actual running pattern in the dog's mind.

While I might use a lightweight one-quarter-inch cord on a little pup, I prefer full-woven three-eighth-inch-line for older dogs. It becomes stiffer with use, and is less likely to hang up on weeds and brush. For the same reason, I don't usually tie a hand loop in the end of the cord. Instead, I tie overhand knots one foot and two feet from the end. While the knots can become wedged between rocks, and other debris, it happens far less frequently than it does with loops. The reason for two knots is, of course, to give me something to grab

Wear gloves to avoid rope burns when training a dog to quarter. Let the check cord run freely through your hands as the dog runs past.

when the cord is scorching through my hand. If I miss the first one, I have a second chance. Be sure to wear gloves when first using the check cord; rope burns can be very painful.

You'll need a large open area in which to begin quartering lessons. Lead the dog to it with the check cord choked up to about leash length. When you're ready to begin, get the knotted end in your hand, release your shorter grip, say ALL RIGHT, and step forward to let Buckshot know it's OK to move out.

When the dog has pulled nearly all of the fifty feet of cord through your hands, blow the long whistle tone, and turn him with the cord.

As the dog runs ahead and nears the end of the check cord, blow a long note on your whistle as described in step 9 of part 1. If he looks back, point your arm in the direction opposite from the one the dog has been running, turn, and walk away from the dog. He'll follow and will soon be racing past you.

As you blow the whistle for TURN, also give the hand signal, and start moving in that new direction yourself. Your dog will quickly pass you and range ahead in preparation for the next turn.

If Buckshot doesn't look back when you whistle, he most certainly will an instant later when he reaches the end of the cord. Be careful what you're doing at that moment. *Do not make eye contact.* He already suspects that you did this somehow. If he catches you staring at him, he'll know it. If he's in doubt, he'll conclude that he jerked his own neck. He'll quickly learn that the whistle precedes the jerk, so he'll "outsmart it" by turning the moment that long tone begins.

It's OK to be facing in Buckshot's general direction so you can see him in your peripheral vision. You'll need to know when to give the arm signal and turn to walk in the opposite direction. Just avoid actual eye contact.

This is the correct way for the choke chain to be positioned on the dog's neck.

Wrong! If the choke chain looks like this, it will continue to choke the dog after you cease the brief jerk. Slide the chain off of the dog's neck, turn it around, and slide it back on again.

For most dogs, it's best to use their ordinary buckled collar while learning to quarter on the cord. If you have a very willful, dominant-type youngster that wants to make it a struggle, it may be necessary to switch to a choke chain for a more emphatic pinch when he hits the end of the cord. If so, be sure the choke chain is fastened correctly. When put on backward, it continues to bind and choke after the tension is released. When fit correctly, it snugs and pinches when you jerk, but releases the instant the jerk ends. In this instance, the dog provides his own jerk when he ignores the whistle and hits the end of the cord. The chain must release, however, when he turns toward you.

When the young dog is learning to quarter, always work into the wind. *Dogs naturally tend to quarter into the wind.* When you return, it will be the dog's natural inclination to run straight downwind, so shorten your grip on the cord to leash length, and lead him back.

The Navy said: Learn this knot; tying yourself to something with a bowline may be the only thing that prevents you from being washed overboard in high seas. I learned it, and never once had to lash myself to the ship, but I sure have put it to good use making leashes and check cords. Practice the first two steps, then put a snap in the lower loop, and pull it snug. Tie a bigger loop on the other end if you want a handhold. Burn the ends so they don't fray.

Always stop quartering while it's still fun for both of you. Don't keep it up until the dog wilts, or he'll decide this game is not fun. Attention span and enthusiasm vary widely between dogs, but try perhaps six turns the first time and then add a couple more with each session. At any sign of the dog going slack, stop, and don't do as many next time.

Brief sessions two or three times a week are all you'll need. When the dog is consistently turning to the whistle, let go of the cord. Let him drag it. If he's still consistent, that's probably all he'll need. If his response to the whistle becomes sloppy later, give him a refresher course.

Step 6

Must Come

While taking fairly long walks a couple times a week, continue to practice quartering with Buckshot dragging the cord. Obviously, he'll be running a lot wider now than when you held the 50-foot check cord, but that's no problem as long as he's turning to the long tone on the whistle. Don't nag him with the whistle at every turn, however, or he'll begin to ignore it. Try to only use it when you want to change your direction of travel.

If your dog hasn't learned COME as a little pup, make it rewarding at first by offering a piece of baked liver or other goody as you blow a staccato on the whistle.

If everything is going well with Buckshot's running pattern, it's time to add COME. Those who started their pups early already have dogs that respond to COME. The pups always did it because they were rewarded for doing so. Now it's time, however, for them to learn that they *must* COME when called.

If you have an untrained yearling, this may be his first introduction to COME. If so, it can't hurt to make it more inviting at first. Bake a hunk of liver, cut it in small pieces, and carry it along in a plastic bag.

Regardless of Buckshot's past training (or lack of it), let him run while dragging the check cord until you've had perhaps two or three opportunities to turn him with the whistle. By that time some of his exuberance has worn off, and he'll probably pay more attention to you. Now watch for a chance to grab the check cord as he runs past. When he's nearly a cord length from you, blow the long tone. As he turns, call "Buckshot, COME!" Always stress the command word with your voice. His name gets his attention; the command tells him what to do.

Dogs that learned COME as pups won't need rewards. Use the check cord to avoid refusal.

As you call, drop to your knees as an added invitation for him to respond. He'll probably start running toward you. If not, haul him in with the cord. Don't get rough about it. Coming to you should never be a bad experience, or he'll start trying to avoid it. Call COME in an inviting and pleasant tone two or three more times as you bring him in. When he gets there—whether voluntarily or not—give him a liver reward and lots of petting and hugs as you ATTABOY him several times.

Those dogs that were taught COME as little pups won't need the liver reward. Just call and they'll come running most of the time. Use the check cord to enforce the command those times when Buckshot decides he'd rather not do it. It's the check cord that's teaching *must* COME.

If you have such a well-behaved young dog that he comes *every* time he's called, you'll have to set up a temptation to make him want to avoid it. If he never has a reason to avoid responding to COME, he'll never learn that he *must* respond to COME. Try calling him just as he's headed toward water for a drink.

The same lesson must be taught to dogs getting liver rewards. The liver is only a temporary bribe to promote quick understanding and response. When the dog knows what COME means, we'll have to phase it out so he can learn *must* COME. As soon as he's responding to the command fairly well, wean him by withholding the treat once every fourth time. Just praise him. During the next week of training withhold every third treat. After that, every second treat. Finally, no treat. At that point the dog knows the command, but sooner or later he'll decide not to obey. That's when you teach *must* COME with the check cord.

When Buckshot is responding to *must* COME every time, you need to add the whistle signal. This signal, like the long tone for TURN, will be distinctive so the dog can easily tell the two apart. We'll blow a *tweet-tweet-tweet* staccato for COME, which is an altogether different sound than the TURN whistle, yet chosen for the same reason. You'll recall that the long tone for TURN is used because it can be continued for a reasonable length of time without feeling the need to punish the dog for ignoring it. The COME staccato can also be continued for a reasonable length of time. If you blew a single, short blast for COME, and the dog didn't instantly respond, you'd have to punish him or lose control. (The short blast is saved for WHOA. With WHOA there's no way to extend the command or the dog would be into the birds. It's either obey this instant or be punished.)

To introduce the whistle, first use the vocal command, then follow it immediately with the staccato. After perhaps 10 or 12 times, the dog is probably beginning to associate COME with the *tweet-tweet-tweet*. Now switch it; whistle first, then order COME. If he comes with the whistle and before the vocal command, he has definitely made the connection. If not, don't worry. He'll soon begin anticipating the COME command following the staccato, and come to the whistle.

Once he's responding well to the whistle/vocal sequence, stop using both signals at the same time. Instead, alternate them and mix them up. Use only one at a time, however, because the dog needs to respond to the whistle while hunting and to the vocal command when you don't happen to have the whistle handy.

Continue practicing both TURN and COME every time you go for a walk, hopefully twice a week. Don't overdo TURN and COME, though, or the dog will feel nagged and ignore you. Praise him whenever he does it right.

When I have a dog that tends to range a little too wide for the density of cover, I say something such as, "Good Boy," every time he swings past. If he runs by within my reach, I also touch him as he passes. Dogs will do this back, often bumping your leg with their shoulder as they run through. I've heard fellows yell, "Watch where you're going, you clumsy ox!" Don't. They're just touching base in their own way. None of this will keep a dog with good instincts from hunting at a decent range, but all of it will help keep the dog a bit closer to you and help him check in regularly.

This dog is not biting. His mouth is the only handlike grip he has, so he uses it to show affection much the way you use your hands to pet him.

A few dogs also touch back by using their mouths as we do our hands. I've noticed this mostly around the yard. I'll free a dog to romp, and he'll race past a few times to show his enthusiastic appreciation. I'll pat his shoulder or rump as he runs by. Some dogs begin to hit my hand or arm with an open mouth as I reach down to pat them. This shocks a few people who think the dog is trying to bite. Quite the contrary; he's patting back with the only thing he has that approximates a human hand.

Dogs on chains also sometimes use their mouths for a light handlike grip on your arm to keep you from leaving. Some animal behaviorists have warned against permitting this, saying, "They're trying to control you—trying to be boss." To me, that's as logical as saying,"Don't let your wife kiss you; she's trying to be dominant."

If Buckshot has been taught to drink from a bottle, reinforce your COME commands with water in the field. If you do this regularly, your dog will be happy to COME when invited.

Another good trick that encourages a dog to check in more often and hunt a bit closer is to carry a plastic soda bottle filled with water. Introduce it on hot, dry days. When his tongue is hanging, call him in. His mouth is already open. Pour some water into it, and he'll immediately learn to lap water coming from a bottle. Obviously, this doesn't work as well on cool days or when surface water is easily available.

Getting back to check-cord training in the field, you'll soon tire of having the dog drag a rope. Keep in mind, however, that snapping this rope to Buckshot's collar has meant he's under control. He knows that, and he probably knows he's not under control when the rope is off. Instead of removing the cord entirely when you feel he no longer needs it, why not cut it in half, or replace it with a 25-footer, or even a 15-foot-length? It's easier to drag and less likely to become tangled in cover (don't tie knots in the end of this one) yet the dog doesn't know that anything has changed regarding control. If things go well, switch to a 6-footer. Eventually, the dog accepts the notion that when the cord is snapped on, he's expected to hunt under control. Finally you can cut the cord down to 2 or 3 feet. Later, if you choose to work birds or hunt without a cord, carry that little one in your pocket. Snap it on as a reminder of control if Buckshot forgets his lessons.

Interestingly, some dogs associate the sound and feel of the snap with the business of hunting so well that a bolt snap can thereafter be used as a signal: "We're going to work now—no foolishness." No cord need be attached to the snap for dogs that pick up on this. It's worth trying.

Caution: After your dog learns to respond quickly to COME, you may become careless about practicing it in the field. Whatever you do, don't neglect it to the point that the only time you call COME is when you're ready to go home. About the second or third time, the dog will conclude that COME really means QUIT, and he's not ready for that. If you use the command several times during a run, he never recognizes which COME ends his fun.

Important: You can further ensure that Buckshot does not connect COME with quitting. Remember that dogs are place learners. If the last COME occurs at the same place each time, that place begins to mean QUIT, and he may refuse to obey. Quit at a different place each time.

Super-important: A dog's attention span usually lasts less than one-quarter minute. When you call Buckshot, pour on the praise and petting for at least 15 seconds, and he'll forget that he responded to COME and will not connect it with leaving the field. It's good insurance even if you always quit at different locations.

A favor, please: Once you have trained Buckshot to the whistle, please use it as infrequently as possible while hunting. It's just awful to hunt with a fellow who sounds like he's directing traffic in midtown Manhattan.

Step 7

Get In

It's a nice touch to be able to command GET IN and watch your dog unhesitatingly jump into the car, water, cage, kennel, or even a patch or briars that you believe may hold birds. Now's the time to teach GET IN and for most of us it takes no extra time.

Teach the dog to stop and/or sit before getting into the car, kennel, or anywhere else. It gives you a chance to clean the mud and burs off first, if necessary.

Say GET IN, and give the hand signal. He probably won't respond this well the first few times. If he doesn't, grab his collar and the base of his tail and help him in.

If your dog stays in a kennel, you have to put him away when you return from training. Do it with the command. Lead him to the kennel or the cage. Stop at the gate. Say "Buckshot GET IN," and throw one arm forward, much as you use your arm for TURN signals. Some dogs naturally follow the motion of your arm and jump right in. If yours doesn't, grip his collar with your other hand and help him along. After a few times, he'll catch on and do it himself.

To speed up the process of learning, don't give him water between leaving the field and kenneling. His waiting water bucket is an extra incentive to follow your command.

It greatly speeds training if his food is waiting inside the cage (or water if he's thirsty).

If it's mealtime when you're returning the dog to his kennel, he learns even faster. Place his food bowl inside the gate or cage before ordering GET IN.

Those owners who keep the dog in the house can arrange a similar situation with his crate. Feed him in there. When the crate is used as his carrier, he'll jump in on command.

I use the words GET IN because that's what I want him to do, and the command comes to my lips naturally. Others use KENNEL or LOAD. Use whatever you like. Your dog doesn't care. Just be consistent and make it natural so you won't have to stop and think what the command is.

Important: Don't bypass the stop before the command. While it doesn't seem necessary when kenneling the dog, it certainly can become necessary when getting in the car to return from hunting. Buckshot is muddy and may be full of cockleburs. Stop gives you a chance to clean him before he dirties the seat.

Also important: Some dogs naturally sit when brought to a stop. That's fine with me, but most bird dogs simply stand as if at WHOA. I don't use the WHOA command to stop them, however. I just bring them to a halt with the leash. I don't want to associate the WHOA command with anything that may tempt them to break. Food and water obviously provides that temptation.

Step 8

Whoa and Heel on Cable

In this book, I'm including training options that you can, or can not do, according to how your particular dog responds. The ground cable is one option. You can train a dog without it. If you are new to this, however, I strongly recommend using the cable. It prevents lots of mistakes in timing—a serious problem for nearly everyone until they've trained several dogs. It also provides control when the amateur doesn't yet know how to get that control. This is particularly important with a dog in the yearling stage when his greatest desire is to be *out* of control. The cable is especially useful, I believe, for those owners who must do much of their training in suburban or city backyards.

Control is essential, especially for the amateur, and more so for those training near traffic. After I told T. E. Scott what a great training tool his ground cable tie-out is, he started training right beside the highway that runs past his business.

The training cable is simply a very strong wear-and-rust-resistant length of aircraft cable staked at both ends by long U-shaped staple stakes. A ring slides up and down the cable and is attached to a short runner cable which in turn is snapped to the dog's collar.

Scott staked an L-shaped cable with cover growing on both sides. No matter what the wind direction, birds can be planted for the dog.

The Scott Company sells these cables. (See appendix for address.) They can be ordered in any size. Although 100 feet of cable will do, a 200-foot-length is much better. Measure your yard space. If you don't have 200 feet in a straight line, don't worry. Can you manage a total of 200 feet in an inverted U-shape around the end of the backyard? If so, you can make corners in a cable; you'll be amazed by how quickly your young dog learns to navigate those corners.

When I wrote *Speed Train Your Own Retriever*, we built little fences in each inside corner of the cable to force the dog to run around the outside of the corners. Obviously, if there was just a post in the corner, his short running cable would tangle.

The fence is still a good idea, but since that book was printed, T. E. Scott found another, even better, idea—in the junkyard! You need one automobile wheel rim for each corner. It can be staked in place through the stud holes. The cable is laid in the V of the rim, pulled fairly tight, and staked at each end. As I said, the dog learns to run along the outside of the corner.

This sequence shows how rapidly dogs negotiate "wheel" corners in the cable. They quickly learn they must run the outside of the corner.

Cable corners are not essential for obedience training, except to provide adequate cable length. A corner does make an L-shaped route that permits us to plant birds that are always upwind of the dog, regardless of wind direction.

Buckshot already knows what WHOA means and has practiced it in two locations: on the drum and beside the drum. The cable will be the third location. In addition, we will introduce HEEL.

Some books and trainers suggest teaching WHOA with COME. They seem to go together easily. Make Buckshot stand at WHOA, call COME, and he learns both. Unfortunately, he also learns that WHOA means "stand anxiously waiting to break from WHOA." That's not what should be in the dog's mind when he's WHOAED on birds.

WHOA is a restrictive command. COME is a release when used in connection with WHOA. Given a choice, the dog will always be more excited about the release than the restriction. Therefore, instead of teaching COME with WHOA, we will use HEEL with WHOA. HEEL is about as restrictive as WHOA and is certainly no more appealing to the dog than WHOA. HEEL will not make the dog anxious to break WHOA, yet the combination will permit us to teach two commands at once.

WHOA Buckshot on the cable just as he learned it on the drum — with a hand signal and an upward pull on the cord.

Walk Buckshot on leash to the ground cable. Snap the short runner cable to his collar, leaving the leash connected as well. With the dog between you and the ground cable, swing your right hand before his face in traffic-cop fashion, command WHOA, and simultaneously bring the leash up with your left hand so he feels that upward pull as he did on and beside the drum. If your dog was taught the silent WHOA and didn't need the drum training, then use the light slap and tug with the leash instead of the upward pull.

Because he already learned it on the drum, you'll quickly be able to walk almost cord length to Buckshot's front.

Circle as you did when Buckshot was on the drum.

Return to Buckshot's side.

Buckshot may or may not obey WHOA in this new location. A lot depends on intelligence and degree of dominance or submissiveness in his character. If he doesn't WHOA, use the leash more sharply as soon as he tries to move. If he's too quick and moves before you can correct him with the leash, pick him up, and plant him back where he was when ordered to WHOA. Give the command again with a measure of insulted authority in your voice. Once more, jerk the leash sharply upward.

If Buckshot isn't responding, he doesn't know WHOA well enough. Go back to WHOA training on and beside the steel drum, until he's ready to WHOA on the cable with no more than a moderate amount of insistence on your part.

If Buckshot does obey WHOA on the cable without a major struggle, let him stand for 20 or 30 seconds, then say HEEL and step forward with your *left* leg. Your left leg is easier for him to see because he's on your left side, and the motion flashing past his eyes will urge him to move along with you.

Of course, Buckshot doesn't yet understand HEEL, so he'll try to run ahead. He can't go far; you have the leash shortened in your grip, and the running cable is holding him on the other side. He's forced to walk a foot or two from your leg. Train him to HEEL at whatever distance seems comfortable for you.

The cable is giving you firm control, so now is the time for your chosen distance to be established and become a habit. (If you talk to a trainer in obedience competition, he'll tell you how many inches from your leg the dog should walk. Ignore him. You're training a hunting dog. One day, you'll want to sneak up on a duck or bird with your dog at HEEL. You don't want Buckshot so close that he'll trip you.)

At this point, HEEL is just something to move the dog so you can again command WHOA. Keep the dog about where you want him to HEEL, but don't make a fuss over it. He'll learn *must* HEEL later.

Your natural inclination is to repeatedly order HEEL because the dog is trying to pull ahead. Don't. He'll tune out nagging. It's OK to repeat the command as you occasionally jerk him back to position, but don't make a big thing of it. Keep it in perspective. HEEL, at this point, is only two things: A reason to make him move so he can be stopped by WHOA; and a Speed-Train tactic to make double use of our time by paving the way for a new command. *WHOA reinforcement is the principal lesson in this step.* Do not confuse the dog by putting emphasis on anything but WHOA.

OK, you have Buckshot walking at HEEL, or trying to surge, or fighting the running cable. Never mind that. Just walk a few feet and command WHOA as you stop. Simultaneously swing your right hand before Buckshot's face, traffic-cop style, and jerk up on the leash. Insist that he stand for another 20 or 30 seconds, then step out again with the HEEL command.

When he has done the HEEL-WHOA sequence often enough that he's standing without attempting to break, tempt him by taking a step to your right. If he holds, take a couple steps to the left. If he breaks, pick him up and unceremoniously return him to the WHOA site. Angrily order WHOA once more. After 30 seconds, try the side steps again.

Practice this as you HEEL and WHOA up and down the cable. As Buckshot improves on WHOA, walk increasingly farther to one side and then the other. Keep adding a few seconds to each WHOA until he's standing steady for at least two minutes. Eventually, you'll be able to circle the dog and keep him at WHOA about as long as you have the patience for it yourself.

Most of you—at least those who did the drum training properly—will advance much more quickly than I'm making it sound. Some intelligently submissive bird dogs learn WHOA so easily and quickly that one can only conclude they have an inherited inclination to WHOA in much the same way that they have the instinct to point. Practice a few minutes every other day.

The most important tools you have in obedience training—a big hug and lots of praise—should be applied after *every* successful exercise.

Step 9

Sitting on Whoa

Some bird dogs simply stand when brought to a halt. Others figure it's foolish to stand when they can sit. The natural sitter is hard to teach WHOA, and the natural stander is hard to teach SIT. Each dog tends to revert to doing what comes naturally, so considerable practice may be necessary.

Few dogs ever sit while pointing wild birds, but I suspect most hunters would accept even that provided the dog was very good at finding birds. Unfortunately, it's usually the less intense dogs that do it. Bird hunters know this and hate to see any dog sitting on point. It's a "point" of embarrassment. (If you'll pardon the pun.)

Correct sitting on WHOA to prevent sitting on point.

The first signs of sitting come during WHOA training. You expect the dog
to stand, and it sits. If you let it go, sooner or later the dog sits while pointing
planted birds. He knows it's a game because he smells your scent with the
bird's. Chances are, you've stretched the lesson a bit too long for the dog's
patience, so he sits to be comfortable while waiting to see if you're ever going to
flush that phony bird.

**A two-point check cord connection works well for curing sitting on WHOA. Snap the
cord around the flanks, then double the cord and shove it through a ring on the dog's
collar.**

Some trainers tie a half-hitch knot around the dog's flanks with the check
cord, then attach the snap end to the collar. If the dog sits, either on WHOA or
while pointing birds, an upward pull on the cord brings his back end up.
Another clever tactic is to arrange the birds and the courses of travel so the dog
ends up pointing while standing in mud puddles. This works great with cold
water on a cold day, not so great on a tongue-lolling hot day. The dog might
even lie down in it.

The double-point connection also helps when you're heeling a dog that tries to spin in order to get away or escape the rigors of training.

Serious sitting problems often show up early in WHOA training, so I usually catch it while working on the drum. If this sitting manifests itself later, I go back to the drum. Either way, I cease snapping the check cord to the collar. Instead, I loop it around the flanks and fasten the bolt snap back onto the cord, so it makes a sliding noose around the flanks.

When I WHOA the dog on the drum now, he can't sit. I do make him WHOA until the dog *tries* to sit, but then I just jerk on my end of the check cord. The cord is over a limb, so the pull is upward. I practice this until the dog stops trying to sit on the drum.

When you command WHOA, use the upward pull as a reminder.

When it's time to practice the HEEL-WHOA sequence, I arrange the check cord for two-point control. First, I snap the noose around the flank. Then I double the cord and slide it through the D-ring, O-ring, or under the collar. Leaving some slack in between, I now have a connection to either collar or flanks. When I order WHOA, I can pull up on the collar connection; if the dog tries to sit, I can jerk up on the flanks. Practice cures the habit before we get back to birds.

Later, in the field, if you have a dog that needs a reminder, just wrap a short cord around the flanks. Its presence is usually enough.

After a while, I don't even need to bother with the second connection. There's usually a very short cord (shorter than a leash) in my pocket. When I command WHOA, I wrap it around the dog's flanks. Or it can be snapped around the flank. Either way, the dog thinks that the second connection is still there. No matter how far I walk from him during WHOA, he doesn't try to sit.

Step 10

Whoa Anywhere

Although he has stopped to the WHOA command at many places along the ground cable, Buckshot may still consider the cable to be a single location. In his mind, he may now believe that he must WHOA on the drum, beside the drum, and on the cable. He may or may not believe that he must obey the command anywhere else. The way to find out, of course, is to try him.

As before, don't expect much from the HEEL command. Even if Buckshot was beginning to learn HEEL on the cable, he probably won't do it very well when only on the check cord or leash. Again, don't give it a lot of attention. HEEL isn't that important, and we'll get to *must* HEEL in time. Concentrate on WHOA.

As usual, step out with your left leg as you command HEEL and start walking across the yard. Go a few steps, and command WHOA. Don't give the upward jerk. Let's see if by now he'll respond only to the voice command. If he doesn't, stop him with the upward jerk and another, but harsher, WHOA!

Repeat the HEEL-WHOA sequence at a great variety of sites so Buckshot knows he must obey it everywhere. Keep trying without the upward jerk until he consistently responds to the voice command alone. While he's on WHOA, walk farther and farther from him on each occasion until you can circle him at the entire length of the check cord. Kick weeds, and throw grass or whatever into the air to further tempt the dog into breaking. If he does, pick him up, and return him with an angry WHOA!

By now, however, another quick WHOA before he moves should stop him from breaking. Just watch for his muscles to tense as a signal that he's about to take off. Often, the rear end dips slightly as the dog gathers his muscles to spring forward. Be quick with a sharp WHOA.

All this practice may seem extreme for one simple command, but it's the *most important control* you have over a bird dog. If you don't get WHOA right, you don't have a bird dog.

The end of the cable is a good place to teach Buckshot to stop on command even if you keep moving. Order WHOA just as the runner cable ring is about to hit the cable stake, and your command will be enforced.

So far, the dog has stopped for WHOA when you stopped. Now he has to learn to stop independently. Go back to the cable. HEEL toward the stake at one end. Just as the ring on the runner cable is about to come to a halt against the stake, command WHOA while you walk another couple of steps. If he stopped on command, go back and say your fondest ATTABOYS. If he didn't stop, the ring hit the stake, and he still came to a sudden and surprising halt.

HEEL-WHOA up and down the cable, and each time you get to the end, keep on walking as you give the command. It doesn't take an intelligent dog long to figure out where the stakes are and that it's either stop or jerk himself by the neck. If the dog is slow catching on, substitute a choke chain for his collar to teach a more impressive lesson.

When Buckshot learns the locations of the end stakes, surprise him with a staple stake over the cable.

Odds are, when the dog learns the stake locations, he'll WHOA there as you walk on, but he won't do it anywhere else along the cable. Don't try it and give him a chance to disobey your order. Instead, drive another U-shaped stake over the cable perhaps 20 feet from one end. Again, you have two places to practice, but the location of one is a surprise. The day after tomorrow, drive that extra stake 20 feet from the other end. The next time, drive it at the middle of the cable. Mix it up. Every time you train there's a stake in a new and unknown place. Very soon the dog knows he must WHOA regardless of whether you stop with him or keep on walking.

I've left the staple stake standing high for this picture; but drive it to the ground so Buckshot won't be quick to understand what caused his surprise.

When he consistently responds to WHOA, it's time to introduce a new surprise. Snap his leash to the stake at one end of the cable, or have a helper hold him. Do this at mealtime. Show him his food, then carry it to the end, just beyond reach, and place it on the ground. Release him. When he races toward the bowl, yell WHOA just before the runner ring hits the stake. If he obeys, walk over, get the bowl, place it within reach, and say ALL RIGHT! Pat and praise him as he eats. If he doesn't obey, HEEL him back to the starting point and try again.

The next time, switch ends of the cable. When he learns at both ends, start shifting the location of a third stake.

Command WHOA just as the ring is about to come to a halt against the staple.

Learning to WHOA at any site and whatever your location is extremely important. It's your control when you see him about to creep on birds. It's even more important for grouse hunters because it's the control which enables them to stop the dog the instant he smells birds. If he does this in practice, he'll learn to freeze the instant he smells grouse in the woods. If he doesn't learn this and tries to get closer, most of the grouse will be gone before the hunter arrives.

Once again, although the dog obeys perfectly on the cable, he may not see the need to obey in another location. No problem. You may have mushroom stakes or spiral stakes left from puppy training. Any stake will do as long as the check cord can't slide over the top. HEEL Buckshot on check cord toward a stake in the ground. Make sure the dog goes past the stake on one side and you on the other. As you go, drop slack cord over the stake and continue walking. Just as the slack is almost used up, command WHOA. Practice HEEL-WHOA around the yard wherever you have the stakes driven.

Use a different tactic with the food bowl. Tie the check cord to a stake, tree or whatever is handy. Walk to the end and choose a site about three feet beyond the cord. Bring Buckshot out on leash and also connect the leash to the tree. When that's done, fasten the check cord snap to his collar. Both check cord and leash are now snapped to his collar. That's important because when he hears and feels you unsnap the leash, he'll forget the check cord is still attached and think he's free.

With Buckshot restrained at the tree or stake, carry his food bowl out to the chosen site. Return, and make sure the check cord is not tangled in any way that could prematurely abort the dog's dash toward his food. Unsnap the leash while saying ALL RIGHT. Say WHOA just as he's about to hit the end of the check cord. Change locations every evening when you feed him in this manner.

Some less gluttonous dogs would rather romp than eat when released from the kennel. If this prevents your dog from accepting food-bowl WHOA training, save table scraps for these occasions. Let the dog smell the scraps before you carry them to the WHOA site. Few dogs can resist that. If yours does, he's probably getting too many scraps. Temporarily withhold them except when WHOA training.

One step remains: WHOA with no restraint. If you've practiced adequately, your dog will probably stop on command. Dogs are like kids; they may test you to see if they can get away with it this time. Once a dog knows you can't catch him to enforce a command, he'll do what he chooses. Watch for it before it happens. Give him his first chance to disobey off the check cord while you're nearby. A marble from a sling shot is a marvelous reminder if the dog bunches his muscles to break WHOA. (Practice with the sling shot first, of course, so you're absolutely sure of being able to hit the rump. You don't want to injure your dog; you want to enforce the lesson.)

Those trainers who can't get the hang of using a sling shot might try a BB pistol. *Don't use a Co² BB pistol.* The BB velocity is too high to be safe. A pumped-air pistol can be regulated to fire a BB with just enough velocity to sting, but not injure. Never use anything in punishment that resembles a shotgun. Once a dog becomes shy of the sight of a gun, you're in deep trouble.

The trick with either a sling shot or air pistol is to use it the first time the dog breaks WHOA. The dog then knows you can reach him even off the check cord and, fortunately, he doesn't understand the limitations of distance.

Hint: The third stake over the cable during WHOA practice must be driven all the way to the ground so the dog can't see it and be forewarned. This also can make it nearly impossible to lift out by hand, but a crowbar or other pry bar used as leverage beneath the stake will lift it easily.

Remember: A dog works more diligently to get praise than he does to avoid discomfort. It's easy to forget that and make training a do-it-or-else deal. Don't. Training proceeds much faster and far more smoothly if you remember to praise everything the dog does right. (This works equally well on mates and children.)

Important: During this yearling phase of training, we have always led Buckshot away from WHOA. We have never released WHOA with ALL RIGHT or COME. This is especially important for those who will teach their dogs to be steady to wing and shot. Our dog never leaves a WHOA site of this own volition, and until he learns to retrieve he won't even leave a WHOA site without us going along, too.

Step 11

Whistle Whoa

Getting tired of WHOA? So am I. Think how Buckshot must feel! Nevertheless, he'd better learn WHOA in one more language: the whistle. There are times when your dog is acting birdy off in the distance on a day when quail are as nervous as a sinner on his death bed. If he won't WHOA, you'll need a rocket to arrive in time to hear the whir of wings. The whistle will get there more emphatically than your voice. In fact, regardless of distance, a whistle signal, if understood, is the best way to command WHOA. It's commanding, and it does not reveal emotion in your voice.

We will use a single, sharp, loud blast. It's forceful, and there's no reason for a longer tirade. If the dog doesn't obey instantly, it's usually too late to stop the flush, anyway.

You can work the whistle in at any time of the WHOA training or practice as long as the dog is consistently performing. If the dog is having trouble learning, though, don't confuse the issue with another way of ordering WHOA. Wait until he understands what to do and understands that it's in his own best interest to do it.

If the dog has had no whistle training on WHOA, go back to the steel drum for quick understanding, then practice beside the drum.

If you've gone all the way through WHOA training without the whistle, you might find it helpful to go back to the steel drum. The drum is a quick teacher. Buckshot already knows what to do. You lift him onto the barrel, and he stands like a statue to keep from sliding off. Now, instead of simply saying WHOA when you raise your hand, blow a single blast first, then order WHOA.

Do this several times during the next week. Also blow the whistle before saying WHOA when you practice beside the drum. The following week, move to the cable. It won't take long before Buckshot recognizes that the WHOA command always follows a sharp whistle blast. He will begin to anticipate the command, and very soon he will stop for the whistle.

Lots of practice in various locations will give you whistle control of WHOA wherever the dog is and whatever he's doing.

After that, it's just a matter of practice. You can do the cable and food-bowl routines, if you like or if the dog seems to need it. Otherwise, after he's responding to the whistle, just practice on the check cord. An intelligent dog catches on to this new command in short order, and accepts it as readily as the voice command. Both ways of ordering WHOA must be used regularly however, or the dog will forget them.

Hint: If you're using a double-ended whistle, you may find the blast from the ball end a little hard to take—neighbors may find it more so. I use the end without the ball for WHOA training, then I try the ball end for a louder blast when the dog is at a distance in the field. Most dogs accept the difference in tone and understand that it's a short blast that still means WHOA. If yours doesn't, do a little practice to ingrain the lesson.

Step 12

Deciding Who's Boss

I warned you earlier that bird dogs reach a stage somewhere between 8 and 14 months of age when adolescent behavior may inspire you to contact the dog pound. Dogs with dominant genes are now becoming pretty sure that they'd make better pack leaders than their masters. Even the submissive types think they know better ways of doing things. Testosterone is making the males more than a little whacky. First heat periods surprise us with character changes in females.

From the yearling dog's point of view, that human they once thought to be a god has lately shown himself to be inept. "Why, he can't even run! He's always plodding along behind," Buckshot thinks. "When he finally does get to the covey point, he can't hit the birds. Sometimes, he just flushes them, and they all get away without a shot! Wouldn't it make more sense to sneak up and pounce on those birds without his clumsy interference?"

Sure enough, the pup that hunted beautifully, almost without training, in his first season, has suddenly become an idiot that can't even accept training without a struggle. You've tried to stay calm because the beatings he deserves will only dull the bird-dog "shine" that you prize so highly. But the tail is wagging the dog here. You've got to get back in control before everything is lost.

Animal behaviorists say we can assume pack leader control in the same ways that some dogs control other dogs. Dogs understand these things so they accept them readily.

You may recall the picture of Buckshot mouthing my hand. Although it appeared to be biting, it was actually a very gentle, affectionate act. Wolf pack leaders do the same thing on subordinates' muzzles. You can imitate this with your hands.

The leader in a wolf pack grips the tops of subordinates' muzzles with his jaws. It's not a viselike grip, but a gentle, almost fondling working of the mouth and head. Nevertheless, there is always the possibility of the pack leader clamping down for enforcement should the subordinate decide to resist this demonstration of superiority.

Not too many of us will grip a nose and muzzle in our own mouths. We don't have to. Dogs sometimes use their mouths to imitate what we do with our hands, and this is one occasion where our hands can be a good substitute for their mouths. Grip the top of your dog's muzzle with your hand, work your fingers to gently fondle, and move the dog's head about slightly in an irregular pattern.

This is an excellent way of reminding your dog that you're still the boss. If he tries to wriggle out of your grip, you know he doesn't believe in your superiority. Make him accept it whether he likes it or not. You can't grin without feeling happier or frown without feeling gloomier. He can't accept your fondling hand without feeling subordinate.

Humans regard the arm over the dog's shoulder as an affectionate gesture. To dogs, it means a test of dominance.

If your dog tries to slip out from under your arm, he's not convinced that you're the pack leader.

Some dogs refuse to eat if you're holding the food bowl. It makes them feel too much like puppies accepting food from their dams. They're too big, too proud, and too determined to overthrow your authority to accept that. Let them get a bit hungrier. It may help them resolve the problem of who is the chief provider. At least one behaviorist spits on the chow to even further simulate food from the dam's mouth. Although this seems new, old-time dog trainers did let dogs lick spittle from their hands when no other reward was handy.

If you've watched a litter of pups that was more than 7 weeks old, you've seen them establishing their pecking order. A favorite way of demonstrating superiority is a front leg, sometimes both legs, placed over another pup's neck. At times, it may just be a paw, or even a head placed over the other's neck. Being physically "above" the other, however, is literally taken as being superior among canines. They may do this to each other until enough tries, threats, and squabbles end the matter, and one accepts the other's dominance.

We can simulate this—and often do because humans regard it as an affectionate gesture—by throwing an arm over our dog's neck and shoulders. If your dog tries to squirm out from under your arm, he's contesting you for top dog position. Don't allow it. Put your arm, even your chin, over his neck on a regular basis from now on.

These moves should help you resume control over your rebellious yearling without damaging the relationship or destroying a large part of the dog's spirit. Be sure to give them a thorough chance to work before trying anything else.

If none of these tactics are getting results, you may have an extremely dominant animal that requires more serious measures. Or, perhaps your dog is about two years old. That's the age when most canines try hardest to assume control over the "pack"—whether it's other dogs, you, or the whole family.

In either case, and assuming you have thoroughly attempted the other moves first, you may want to try something weird and unproven that just may work. Urine holds great importance for canines. They mark territories, advertise sexual readiness, express fear, and show dominance through how it's used and the odors involved. Trainer Bruce Ludwig told me that his old Irish setter, on two different occasions, cocked his leg and filled the boots of hunters who had repeatedly missed the birds he had pointed. It would be difficult to find a clearer way to express the superiority that this dog felt over the humans during those moments.

Telling your dog, in that manner, that he's subordinate may be effective. It also may be socially unacceptable in your neighborhood. Instead, you may want to collect a specimen in a squirt bottle that is free of other odors (such as soap). Squirt the dog's shoulders to see if it will help to modify his rebellious behavior.

Probably the most dramatic response to urine that I've encountered was with Peat, a 2-year-old Gordon setter that was threatening my friend, Dan Thomason's new wife Karen. I, too, had a confrontation with Peat while hunting forest grouse with Dan, but what I did (I'll get to that in a moment) couldn't be done to a dog this large by 89-pound Karen. I suggested the urine treatment. Soon after I returned home, a letter from Dan described a different kind of scene in which Karen was now rolling on the living room floor with a big, docile bird dog.

Dan has since recommended the urine method to five friends with unruly, dominant dogs of various breeds. Four were permanently successful. The fifth found that he had to repeat the treatment every two weeks, otherwise his dog's dominant, aggressive nature would resurface.

What I did with Peat was the most dominating of all canine behaviors, except for an all-out battle of teeth. Please understand that this Gordon setter was not an incorrigible renegade. He was an excellent, highly intelligent grouse dog that was simply going through the two-year-old stage in a rather extreme way, as some of the brighter canines do. A reversal of behavior had to be started soon, however, or the dog's dominant manner would become habitual and increasingly difficult to change. Peat and Dan had a marvelously companionable relationship until this time, so Dan was wisely avoiding the beatings that onlookers were suggesting. The side effect of beatings could have been the loss of those qualities Dan prized most in his dog.

On this particular day, it's probable that Peat resented my intrusion into the one-on-one hunting relationship that he usually enjoyed with his master. Dan shot a grouse, and when Peat neither retrieved nor came back, we went to look. Lots of feathers lay where the bird hit the ground—or was held down to get a better grip. Either Peat hid the bird (perhaps because of my presence) or the bird ran off. I thought we should give Peat the benefit of the doubt and try to get him to take the trail in case the bird did run off.

Dan held the Gordon's nose close to the feathers and ordered him to find the bird. Peat made one cursory look and headed past me to resume hunting. I thought he should try harder than that, so I reached down to grab his collar to bring him back for another try.

Peat was accepting no such handling from a subordinate. He swung his head around, mouth open, and smacked me with a fang on the end of my nose hard enough to break skin and draw blood. He didn't mean to eat my face, or he would have. It was only a warning. My response was automatic and without thought. I already had the collar by one hand, so I tackled Peat, grabbing his muzzle with my other hand on the way down. We landed with my body holding his to the ground. I growled viciously into his ear. He growled back and struggled so hard I could scarcely hang onto the muzzle. We kept this up until he stopped growling back.

When I got up—carefully, by the way—Peat remained on the ground, eyes rolling, for a full two minutes by my watch. When he stood, I put my arm over his shoulder to show that dominance would continue, but I also talked quietly to indicate that we'd hold no grudges.

Fortunately, Dan (standing there with a shotgun) understood what I was doing. Dan and Karen continued to demonstrate their dominance after I left. Peat's bid for pack leader status was resolved without a single beating, without diminishing any of the Gordon's fine qualities as a hunter and companion, and without creating other problems that would require more time to correct.

Had this been a dog of mine attempting dominance, it would have been much easier. I would have done a dominant "lay-over" under much less threatening circumstances and I would have tried all the other moves before the lay-over. If it finally came down to a lay-over, I *wouldn't* have taken a dive at the dog. I would have held him by the collar for control, and I'd have reached under his belly to grab an opposite foot, (both if I could manage it), and pull them toward me to flip the dog on its side. I'd be on top before he could scramble, and as before, my second hand would be quickly gripping the muzzle both for my own protection and as another show of dominance.

The dominant lay-over is very threatening to the dog and should only be attempted by professionals.

A warning: A lay-over on any dog, but especially one that is as suddenly and as aggressively performed as that I gave to the Gordon, is about as safe to the amateur dogman as wresting alligators. Unless you're a pro at avoiding teeth, *don't do it!* If you try it, I don't want to hear about the tooth marks.

Important: These behavioral moves are all intended to deal with a dog that's making a bid for dominance. They're not shortcuts that will eliminate the need for adequate training. Each phase of training requires an introduction that the dog understands and enough repetitions to prevent him from forgetting. If, after that, the dog defies you because he's struggling for dominance, then, yes, you'll have his attention once you prove to him that you are top dog.

One amateur who read about the dominance moves was having a training problem with a Brittany, a problem which had nothing to do with a struggle for supremacy. He thought, however, that dominance moves would speed up the training. On top of that he skipped the milder moves and went directly to the lay-over, which is as severe as it gets in canine language, short of biting your dog.

Except for some field-trial Britts with pointer genes crossed in, Brittanys are rarely very dominant. A bigger problem is their habit of acting like they're about to die if you even pinch their ears. And that's how this dog reacted. It was scared to death by the lay-over, and confused as well. The lay-over came as a bolt out of the blue that the dog couldn't understand. All the Brittany got out of it was that her master is unstable. That fellow suddenly and grossly magnified his training problem.

Make sure it's a bid for dominance that you're dealing with, not a lack of your training effort. If in doubt never use the most severe measure first.

Step 13

Gun Conditioning

Those who did the little puppy training probably breezed through gunfire introduction as if it couldn't be a problem. Little children and small pups tend to accept the lifestyle of their particular family as "normal," even when bizarre. The unnaturally loud blasts of gunfire are accepted as normal far more easily by puppies than by older dogs, especially if the noise is associated with something exciting like birds.

On the other hand, if your dog is 5 to 8 months old, sometimes even a little older, he might be going through a weird stage – quite opposite from the little puppy stage – in which he could place all the wrong interpretations on gunfire. One day you may notice that anything which so much as seems unusual or different is regarded as threatening. A friend comes to visit, and the pup runs to hide or barks in fear. The pup has seen you a thousand times, but one day he's sure you're an intruder. If the wind is from him to you, and he can't identify you by odor, a kenneled dog may act threatening right up to the moment you let him sniff your hand. You can be talking to him the whole while and he doesn't correlate it with the person who has fed him his entire life. My wife recalls that babies go through a similar stage of fearing strangers and burying their faces into their mothers' necks in attempts to hide.

Individual pups (and children) vary widely in how extreme their behavior becomes during this period. Some breeze through it; others seem downright goofy. Don't worry. They'll outgrow it. If your pup is in this stage and already spooky of everything, however, this is no time to introduce the shotgun. Wait until this strange stage has ended.

Place a shotgun next to the food bowl so the sight of your gun isn't regarded as threatening.

If the dog doesn't even notice the gun, smear something good smelling on the stock.

Just so the sight of a shotgun isn't regarded as threatening I like to place some kind of long arm beside the food bowl while the pup eats. He may not even notice it. In that case, I smear some gravy on the stock. He'll smell it and lick it off. After a few times, he'll see the gun as good news, and that's the way it should be.

Lots of trainers fire a gun to signal mealtime. They start with low power .22 shorts, then gradually advance through the more powerful .22s, and on to the shotgun. Sometimes they target practice while the dog eats.

Unfortunately, firing at mealtimes is not an option for many owner-trainers. In some municipalities, discharging a BB gun is even illegal. If legal, though, it's something to start with. At first, use the air rifle or spring-loaded BB gun empty, then after a few days load and fire it, so the noise produced is somewhat louder.

Cap pistols ordinarily can be fired in town, but also have a long arm in your hand so the dog associates the gun with the report. Toy rifles that shoot ping-pong balls sometimes make more noise than cap guns.

For a louder report, you might experiment with different materials slapped together. A pair of wooden paddles makes a good report. Try different lengths and widths to achieve the right sound. A pair of 24-inch, heavy-metal drywall trowels make an even louder, sharper report. A ¾-inch board slapped against the flat, solid metal surface of a table saw makes a sound similar to that of a rifle. I'm not suggesting anyone use a saw for that purpose, but you might look for a large, heavy-metal surface to slap with a length of board. Experiment. Whatever you decide to use, let your neighbors know in advance so they don't become nervous.

Working the action of a shotgun as the dog eats will help him accept sudden unusual noises.

A Master's Voice Gunshy Cure or Prevention tape is the easiest, most effective way to desensitize the dog to shotgun blasts.

Working the action of a shotgun while the dog eats is also a noise that's helpful for training in town.

By far the easiest and most effective introduction to the sounds of shotguns is the Gunshy Prevention tape sold by Master's Voice. (See appendix for address.) Much like the Gunshy Cure tape, the prevention recording begins with soothing music. Shotgun reports are added almost imperceptibly in the second segment. Gradually, segment after segment, the shotgun becomes louder until it equals the music in volume. After that, the shotgun blasts remain loud while the music diminishes with each succeeding segment. At last, nothing is heard but the shotgun. By that time, the dog thinks gunfire is as soothing as the music was in the beginning. The tape is especially effective if used while feeding or while the dog is doing anything else he really enjoys.

Even in the country, the tape is the most effective gunfire introduction. Those persons who don't care to buy the tape can start with .22 shotshells or with shotgun shells with the crimp cut off and the lead removed. Both are very mild reports that are easily accepted by dogs. Gradually advance through .22 shorts, then longs and long rifles (low velocity, then high) in a rifle. After that, go through the same sequence in a .22 pistol for louder reports. Also carry a rifle or shotgun for sight association, of course. Finally, fire the shotgun at a distance and move gradually closer with each succeeding shot. Again, this is most effective if done while the dog is enjoying himself in some special way such as eating.

Most dogs can advance faster than I've suggested here, but there's no sense risking problems. Once you've made a dog gun-shy, you're in serious trouble. If at some point you should happen to notice noise sensitivity in your dog (for example, fear of thunder, firecrackers, and so on), I would strongly recommend that you stop right there and order a Gunshy Prevention tape. Noise sensitivity is an inherited propensity that requires desensitizing. Without that, the odds are strong that you'll eventually end up with a gun-shy dog.

Tip: After the dog is accustomed to gunfire, take the shotgun along on walks in the field, especially if you intend your dog to be steady to shot. Fire randomly and fairly often. If the dog runs back to see what's going on, he finds that nothing has. Before long, he concludes that most gunfire is of no consequence to him, so he begins to ignore it. He's now much easier to steady.

Step 14

Back to Birds

If you started Buckshot as a puppy, he got a good grounding in birds. Then he reached the age when trying things his own way made you stop bird work until he became old enough to accept serious obedience training. If, for whatever reason, you started Buckshot later, you developed his enthusiasm for birds, maybe even allowed some chasing. Once he developed the desire to hunt, you too had to quit until Buckshot could be brought under firm WHOA control. Assuming that your dog is now conditioned to the gun and responds perfectly to WHOA, it's time to resume bird work in a new way.

Up until now, we planted the birds and brought the dog into the vicinity on a check cord. Whether started as a puppy or older, our dog soon learned that our scent was always with the bird. He realized that this was a game. Perhaps his tail began flagging back and forth on point. Eventually, the dog may have decided to improve his part in the game by trying to catch the bird himself.

From now on, we have to convince Buckshot that this is no game. In the old days, it was easy. There were plenty of wild birds. When the dog was switched from planted to wild birds – if he ever was worked on planted birds – he quickly learned that he couldn't catch critters that fly. If he crept too close, they flew. He learned that it takes a cooperative master-and-dog effort to catch a bird, so he started holding his points.

We can approximate the wild-bird experience with recall quail. These are still pen-raised birds, however. They don't smell exactly like wild quail because their diets are different. That fact was long suspected, but lately it has been proven by bloodhounds in police work. Bloodhounds can recognize the difference between my blood odor and yours, for example, but they may think yours is your child's or the reverse. When this was proven in the field, an Illinois laboratory broke blood into several components which were then used to retest the hounds. These hounds recognized individuals only in the blood component that contained the wastes – the part that differs because of diet and environment. Again, bloodhounds couldn't tell the difference between a father's blood and his son's, but they knew the difference between blood wastes of all individuals not living in the same household.

While recall quail do not smell exactly like wild quail, the more important fact is that we don't have to plant these birds, so our own scent is not found either on the quail or around the site. The dog is not as likely to recognize that we are playing a training game. The birds are free to fly and they will if the dog tries to creep too close.

Buckshot soon realizes that he must "handle" these birds. He'll never catch one without your help. This doesn't mean that recall quail can make up for lack of WHOA training, however. If your dog's pointing instinct isn't very strong, and his desire to please also lacks strength, he may be quite content to accept flushing and chasing as his reward for finding the birds. The moment the dog points, you must be able to hold him with the WHOA command. Do your WHOA training well in advance of bird work. Never try to turn a dog's point into a WHOA lesson. Trying to teach WHOA in the presence of birds is too much pressure on the dog, and the resulting hassle will set your training back for weeks.

You need to check Buckshot's willingness to hold before letting him run free to hunt recall quail. You will control him with a check cord, but you have to "plant" the bird without leaving your body scent at the plant site.

If your training area is relatively free of trees, a two-liter soda bottle fastened to a pigeon's legs is a good way to "plant" a free flying bird. Use yarn, not string, to tie the bottle to the live bird. First, tie a short piece of yarn from one foot to the other. Then tie the long length of yarn to the short piece. This prevents excessive pull on a single leg.

There are a couple of ways to "plant" a free-flying bird. One is to tie a two-liter plastic soda bottle to the legs of a pigeon with an 18-inch length of yarn. (Yarn doesn't cut; string will.) Throw the bird so it can fly downwind over an open field with moderate cover. (If you throw it into the wind, it will turn and fly downwind, anyway, because it's easier.) When the weight of the bottle brings the bird down, wait a few minutes for scent to accumulate in the area, then circle around and come back into the wind with Buckshot on a check cord.

You may want to try planting the bird ahead of time to see how far yours will fly. If necessary, add a little water to weight the bottle so the bird will be brought down before it can fly to a tree. That happened to me the first time I tried this method, and it can be a hassle. A pigeon flew to a big, old walnut tree and tried to land on a high limb. Of course, the bottle swung down as the bird slowed, so it hooked underneath a limb ahead of the one the pigeon intended to land on. That abruptly brought my pigeon to a halt with the yarn draped over the limb and bird and bottle hanging on opposite sides.

When I went inside for a scoped .22 rifle, my wife asked what was going on. I told her what had happened. "So, you're going to kill the pigeon?"

"Of course not," I boasted. "I'm going to shoot the string."

I don't know why a man does these things, especially when his wife has the time to go along and watch. I grabbed a box of 50 cartridges, figuring I'd bragged myself into wasting the rest of the afternoon. I pulled the trigger on the first cartridge, and to my utter amazement, the bottle fell, and the pigeon flew. The hardest part was keeping my jaw from dropping open and admitting how accidental this had been. I don't care to try it again, and hopefully, you can benefit from my mistake and not get a bird hung up the first try.

Some of you may prefer to use a quail. If yours aren't yet flight conditioned, just tie about two feet of bright yarn to the bird's foot so it is easier to see in case the dog has trouble scenting. For stronger flying quail, tie a plastic coffee-can lid to the yarn. Quail fly lower than pigeons, so there's less chance of one hanging high in a tree.

If you haven't done a good job on WHOA training. Buckshot will break point and try to catch the bird. It's back to the drum for more WHOA practice, this time with a bird in a Scott harness or a mesh bag.

As soon as Buckshot points, whistle or call WHOA. If you use the voice command, don't yell. Make it sound matter-of-fact. Grip the check cord for guarantees. If he ignores the command and breaks, don't say another word. Just do an about-face and brace yourself for the impact of Buckshot hitting the end of the cord. Don't be making eye contact when he does his midair flip.

I know you have heard, or will hear, that a dog should never associate punishment with birds. That's true, but this flip on the check cord is OK. The bird didn't do it. He disobeyed WHOA. If you keep your mouth shut and don't make eye contact, it's doubtful that he'll blame you.

After flipping a few times, your dog may decide to stop punishing himself and start obeying the WHOA command. But don't take this for granted. If Buckshot broke WHOA the first time on birds, you haven't taught the command thoroughly enough. Back to the drawing board—or rather the steel drum—but this time with birds.

The Scott harness keeps the bird immobile without damage to its feathers.

I restrain a pigeon with a harness. You could also place the bird in a mesh bag (such as an onion or orange bag from the grocery store). Throw another cord over the limb several feet beyond the dog. If you're using a swing set, position the dog at one end and the bird at the other. Put the bird on the ground behind a small pile of weeds or brush for camouflage.

It's best if, during this first session, the wind doesn't blow bird scent toward the dog on the drum. The unexpected sight of the raised bird will have more shock value if the dog isn't tipped off by the scent.

WHOA Buckshot on the drum for a least a full minute. Then slowly pull the cord to raise the bird to the dog's eye level. He knows what will happen if he breaks WHOA on the drum, and you know what to do if he tries it.

Practice this once a day until he seems ready to accept standing at WHOA on the drum without attempting to break and catch the bird. Now switch to a greater temptation. Using the pole (with rubber band and ring) as in puppy training, plant the pigeon behind the camouflage (or use a spring-open launcher). As usual, place the dog on the drum and give the WHOA command. Control him with the check cord, and walk forward, pretending to kick cover to flush a bird. Your action will initiate excitement, and flushing the bird will complete it. Again, practice until the dog stops trying to break WHOA.

Also, if need be, practice WHOA off the drum until you can stop your dog with the whistle when he's running free. While you're doing this, you can set up the recall system described in the next step.

A point about points: Apparently, the human critter hates men with shirttails out of their pants, women with a hair or two out of place, and dogs with sloppy points. At least, we spend a lot of time trying to tidy up these things. In the case of dogs on point, we're always after the tail. Raise it. Stroke its underside. Rub gently against the lay of the hair. These actions may serve as reminders to a class dog whose mind wanders because he's somewhat bored by bird games, but it's doubtful that tail-set dictated by genes will be much influenced by manipulation.

Conversely, staunchness and intensity can be improved by handling the dog on point. Push gently against the rump. It sets up an opposition reflex that makes the dog resist forward motion, even when he'd like to jump in on those birds. Let him settle back, then grip the root of his tail and gently raise his rear end off the ground. Some trainers pick the dog up by collar and tail and turn him away from the birds—then back again—slowly, of course. Dogs see this attention as a reward for their work. While angry WHOAs might wilt the dog, handling makes them enjoy their work and appear more intense on point.

Step 15

Controlled Covey of Quail

Quail are covey birds with a strong desire to regroup when scattered. We're all familiar with the *bob-white* or *bob-bob-white* whistle, but that's the cock's call to lure a hen, or to stake his territory once mated. The whistles more important to us are the *werrr-la-he* and *whirl-key* assembly calls. If we keep one quail in a small cage, and release the rest, that bird will harangue about his lonesome condition until all his buddies are back to the cage. If a funnel-shaped tunnel is built into a side of the cage, they'll enter to rejoin him, the food, and the water, and be unable to get back outside. These cages are placed where needed for training and brought back home for the night.

Small portable recall cages can house a controlled covey of about twelve quail.

Portable recall cages must be small, but each can house a dozen or so birds. I use a very simple cage, the top, bottom, and sides of which are made from a 61-inch length of 36-inch wide 1-by-2-inch welded wire. Make the bends around the edge of a board so the wire doesn't buckle in the wrong places. Form 90-degree bends at 20 inches, then 10, then 20 again, and finally bend down the last 11. Bend the 1-inch ends of wires (created when cutting the 61-inch length from a roll) around the horizontal wire on the bottom and crimp tightly to hold the box shape. Cut 10-by-20-inch (plus the raw ends of wires) pieces for the ends and crimp them in place the same way. Cut a 5-by-6-inch opening in the top for access, and fasten a wooden door over it. A 5-inch hole for the funnel could be anywhere on one end, but I chose the middle. I feed the quail from a small crock which can be shoved under the tunnel to keep the birds out of the feed and reduce waste. The tunnel is of ½-by-½-inch mesh. It is 10 inches long, 5 inches in diameter at one end, and 3 inches at the narrow end. A cover over the funnel is necessary to keep small predators from reaching the birds.

These small cages are not dog or coyoteproof, so they shouldn't be left out overnight. Plan on waiting until dark for all birds to recall. You'll lose some quail here and there for one reason or another, but you'll have working coveys for a long time.

Buy birds that are 12 to 16 weeks old. Keep them in their cage for two weeks so they become accustomed to eating, drinking, and living in it. It's home. Then, one after another, grab each bird and place it in the open end of the funnel. They'll run through and jump back into the cage. You'll miss some and do others twice, but don't worry. Monkey see, monkey do. They're learning.

The next step is best done in a vacant, or fairly empty, room such as a garage or shed. Remove half of the birds, and leave the funnel open so they can recall when ready. Do this every day for a few days. Then choose a cock (the best, loudest caller if you can identify him) and leave him in the cage after releasing all the others. After practicing this recall a few times in the room, you're ready to do it outdoors. Play it safe by practicing a few times in somewhat different locations, but without any dog training. After you're sure the birds will recall readily, you can disturb them without losing a bunch. Even so, be careful at this age. Pen raised quail are not usually conditioned to strong flight. Control your dog so he doesn't catch *any*. Just one catch will set you back for weeks while you try to convince Buckshot that it was a fluke, won't happen again, and he should stop trying.

As the quail grow older, they'll fly better, and farther. It's unlikely that Buckshot will catch them. Avoid pushing them more than one-quarter mile from the recall cage while training. If they are too far out, and can't hear the cocks, they won't recall. Even wild quail only have a range of about one-quarter mile.

If you are using birds of the year, you won't lose many to the mating process. After they mature at about a year, however, they pair off and go make a nest instead of recalling to the cage. This can be minimized by releasing only cocks. The lure of the opposite sex back in the cage will bring them home, unless they happen to meet a potential mate in the wild.

Obviously, the recall pen should be placed in the shade. Quail can't take much direct sun, and if your recall bird dies, none of your controlled covey birds will return.

The uptilting mesh-wire funnel allows entry for outside birds, but stops inside birds from getting out. Keep a cover over the funnel at night to keep small predators out.

Pen-raised quail are also easily lost to rain. They haven't learned to pull oil over their feathers from their tail glands, so they become soaked to the skin and die of exposure. If you train on a wet day, cover the recall cage with a piece of plywood. If you plan to release any birds to the wild after training, condition them to use their glands by daily light sprinkling with a hose until they learn. Do this on warm dry days, of course.

Some states won't allow you to capture game birds from the wild, never mind the fact that they were yours in the first place. Check your laws. In those states, you can have a controlled covey by building a sturdy, dog–coyote-proof cage and placing it permanently in a fairly wind-sheltered, shady spot. This cage must not have a recall funnel, but it should have a roof, and a little house on one end.

After the birds have lived in their outdoor location for two weeks, catch your best caller, put him in a little holding cage, and open the door for the others. Don't chase the birds out. Just walk off and leave them, but set up food and water near the cage. They'll wander out, hang around for a time, then gradually widen their territory. When they're far enough away that you won't spook them into flight, return your recall bird to the main cage. The food and water will hold your controlled covey in the area, and they're always drawn to the recall bird in the evening. You'll have the cage closed, of course, but your covey will hang around where you want it throughout their first year or so. After that, if you still need a covey for training, you'll have to buy new birds, and start over. Never mix new birds with old. They'll fight, and the new ones won't recall to that kind of welcome.

Obviously, you'll lose more birds to predation with this system than when the quail are caged at night. If stray dogs or coyotes are a serious problem, a hog wire-mesh fence around the cage area helps. You need a tighter mesh, plus a roof over the fenced area to keep raccoons out. Mink will get into just about everything.

The early permanent recall pens all had two large compartments with houses on both ends and a funnel to each compartment. Half of the birds were kept in each. One end could be opened one day, and the other the next. Half were always in one compartment to recall the birds into the other. (Where recalling is legal, of course.) The problem was that the pen-raised birds weren't flight conditioned, and it took considerable time for them to get that way. Until they were conditioned, there was always the chance of the dog catching one.

The latest development in controlled coveys will condition the birds to flight right in the cage. The affair looks like a well ventilated plywood out-

My quail tower is portable but tall, and it conditions birds to almost straight-up flight. Note the quail running around the base looking for the entrance.

house. It has a door in the front to care for the birds and/or release some. As with any recall cage, it has a funnel near the bottom, covered at night to keep predators out. Up near the roof, a foot or so is open, but wire covered for protection. Shelves are installed around the inside of the upper cage, just below the wire. The quail eat and drink on the floor of one-half-inch mesh wire where they're protected from everything. To sun themselves or just watch the world go by, however, they must fly up to the shelves. Flying up and down flight-conditions the birds.

An added plus to conditioning in this cage is the fact that flight is, by necessity, almost vertical. When released for training and flushed after a dog points, these birds tend to rise in the vertical manner in which they've become accustomed. Remember our ring-and-rubber-band pigeon pole release in Part 1? Because we released vertically, little Buckshot stood and watched instead of chasing. When birds hug the ground, they appear easy to catch, and dogs want to chase. Because of this new development in recalling, we can now also minimize the dog's desire to chase quail.

The one thing about the new recall pens that I object to is their size and weight. It takes a tractor to drag one around, and not everyone can get permission to permanently place this small building on someone's land. Maybe you won't want it in one permanent place because it might be more effective if occasionally moved. Unless you have more than one such pen, you'd have to train on the same one-quarter-mile radius area every time.

I decided to build a sort of quail tower instead. It's 2-by-2-feet at the bottom instead of 4-by-4, so it's 4-square feet instead of 16. That means it can handle only one-fourth the number of birds (a dozen at most) but it's light enough for two people to carry and is easily transported by pick-up truck or tied to the top of a car. With large lawnmower wheels bolted to two bottom corners, it could be pulled to a new location by one person. It's 9 feet tall compared to 6 feet in current models, so the birds are also conditioned to higher vertical take-offs. The smaller area of the tower confines the flight to even tighter straight-up flight. A hinged roof opens, the birds are spooked out the top, and even more emphasis is given to upward flight. This flight habit can be extremely helpful in training dogs to be steady to flush.

As always, at least one recall bird has to remain behind. Simply drop the hinged roof before all the quail have flown out.

As with any recall cage, the quail tower has to be placed in the shade. A tall narrow structure won't stand by itself, especially in wind, so tie or chain it to a fence post or tree. Be sure to trim away any limbs that may interfere with the quails' flight out of the tower.

If you provide food and water in small crocks there is enough floor space for those containers plus the dozen quail. You'll have to care for the birds daily, however. Some of us live too far away and can only tend the birds once or twice a week. If the birds are safe from predators and vandals, that isn't too bad. Quail stay wilder if humans aren't frequently around. It does mean your tower needs more floor space, however. This is easily accomplished by building a sidecarlike detachable addition.

The addition does not make the tower heavier or more awkward to carry because it's detachable. Make the addition the same width as the tower, and as long as necessary for your large food and water containers. If you add another two feet or more in length besides that, you can also double the number of quail kept in your tower.

Pay heed to the following instructions, and do not "improve" upon the design by adding a window for more light, either in the tower or the addition. Both have wire floors, and both are blocked off the ground by bricks or chunks of treated wood, so there's enough light for the birds to feed. Adding a window would only discourage flight conditioning in the tower. There's less incentive to fly to the top if they can gawk at the world through a conveniently low window.

This is a quail's eye view of the tower looking up from the bottom toward the resting shelves and showing the simple 2-by-2 and plywood construction.

Building the quail tower

I built my first tower with one-quarter-inch outdoor quality plywood for lightness, but that also made it a tad flimsy. If you're concerned about a large predator endangering the birds, use one-half-inch plywood. Start with two sheets that measure 8 feet long by 4 feet wide. Cut each down the middle, so you now have four pieces that are 8 feet long and about 2 feet wide. Next, cut four 2-by-2s that are 8 feet 10½ inches long.

You'll have a straight factory edge on each piece of plywood, plus the edge you cut which may or may not be straight. Nail a 2-by-2 along the factory edge of each piece of plywood. Position the 2-by-2s 1½ inches up from the bottom of the sheets of plywood. That leaves 12 inches of 2-by-2 extending over the top of each piece of plywood. Make sure they're all identical. In other words, if one 2-by-2 is nailed to the right hand edge of the plywood, then nail all the 2-by-2s to the right edges.

The lower end view shows construction of the access door and the screened frame that will become the bottom of the tower.

The top end of the tower with the roof opened shows more of the 2-by-2 and shelf constructions.

Now nail the left edge of one sheet to the 2-by-2 of another. Do this three more times, and you have a rather shaky long box. One end has 2-by-2s sticking out. Square up the other end with a carpenter's square, hold it in position, and measure the distance across the inside of the top of that end. Do the same for the inside of bottom. Cut 2-by-2s to these lengths. Shove them in place, then measure the distance between them at each end. Cut 2-by-2s to these lengths. Shove them in place. If they fit, you now have the makings of a frame that shoves into the bottom of the long box and fills the space left by nailing the long 2-by-2s 1½ inches up from the bottom. Remove the short 2-by-2s, (remember their positions), and with just one nail in each corner, finish the frame. Cut one-half-inch wire mesh slightly smaller than the frame, and fasten it in place with small wire staples. The bottom of the quail tower is now finished. Push it in place to help keep the box square, but don't nail it in yet.

Next, measure and cut two 3½-inch wide shelves with notches in the corners so they fit over the 2-by-2s. Cut two more 3½-inch shelves to fit over the ends of the first two, but only as far as the 2-by-2s. Nail these shelves to the first two, forming a shelving frame that will go around the inside of the top end of the box, just below the edges of the plywood sides. Cut two 2-by-2s to be screwed to the inside of the box just under the two lower of the four pieces of shelving. Screw through the outside of the plywood box and into the 2-by-2 instead of vice versa for better strength. Screw the shelving to the 2-by-2s, squaring that end of the long box as you do so.

The roof is of three-quarter-inch plywood, doubled on the front edge for more weight to ensure quick, secure closing.

Measure the distance between the 2-by-2s protruding out of the top end. Cut 2-by-2s to these lengths, and fasten them in place with one nail at each end to complete the framing.

To cover the framing with one-half-inch mesh wire, measure the outside perimeter of the plywood box, *not* the 2-by-2 framing. Cut the wire to the measured length and about 13 inches wide. Place the factory or uncut edge near the top of the 2-by-2 framing. The raw or cut edge will overlap onto the plywood. This will cause the wire to bunch and crimp at the outside corners because the box is bigger than the frame. Don't worry about it. You're not building a cathedral, and being able to staple the overlapping wire onto the plywood greatly strengthens that end of the tower.

The roof or lid should be a little oversized to keep some of the rain out. I used three-quarter-inch-plywood and even doubled that thickness with an extra piece nailed to the front half. The additional weight helps close it faster when the quail are leaving. Hinge the backside with 3-inch strap hinges and add a chain screwed to the front. A length of one-half-inch electrical conduit bolted to the chain will be added later to lift the lid to release birds.

Make a funnel of half-inch wire mesh 10 inches long, and staple it into a 5-inch hole in a piece of three-quarter-inch plywood.

Cut a 5-inch diameter hole in the rear right side of the tower's bottom. The bottom of the hole should be about 6 inches from the bottom of the plywood panel. Now cut a 10-by-12-inch piece of scrap three-quarter-inch plywood to frame and strengthen the hole. Hold the plywood over the hole in the tower, and scribe the circle onto the three-quarter-inch piece.

Build a door to cover the entrance funnel. The funnel will slide into the 5-inch hole, the bottom of which should be 6 inches above the bottom of the tower. (The carpenter placed this hole too low, so the unit had to be reconstructed.)

Cut a piece of one-half-inch mesh wire about 16 inches wide plus the raw wire ends. Cut it 10 inches long to make the length of the entrance funnel. Wrap the wire into a cone 5 inches in diameter at one end and 3 inches in diameter at the other. The 5-inch diameter will be stapled into the 5-inch hole in the ¾-inch plywood. A dog-food can is just the right size to use as a form for the 3-inch end. The cone should be lopsided instead of evenly tapered. When the assembly is inserted into the hole, the top of the funnel should be as close to level as possible. The bottom of the funnel should taper upward. This makes the 3-inch end higher from the floor and harder for quail to jump into and get back out.

The door and funnel assembly in place (although too low on the tower).

When the wire cone is stapled in place, cut a 9-by-10-inch door to cover the opening and keep small predators such as weasels or mink from entering at night. I used 3-inch strap hinges because they're easy to stick in a vise and hammer into the shape necessary to go around the bottom of the three-quarter-inch door. A 4½-inch hasp, also hammered and bent to the necessary shape was installed so the cover door could be locked in place.

The assembled entrance with the door closed.

When the entire funnel assembly is finished, slide it into place, and fasten it by screws driven from inside the tower box onto the three-quarter-inch frame.

Cut a 9-by-16-inch access hole in the front so you can feed and water the birds. The bottom of the opening can be 5 or 6 inches from the bottom of the tower panel. Cover the opening with a 9-by-22-inch plywood door. Again, use 3-inch strap hinges and a 4½-inch hasp, both bent to appropriate shapes. It's important that the hinges are positioned at the bottom of the door. If placed on top, the door will open only part way and obstruct your vision when trying to feed the birds.

With everything installed and no further need to get into the bottom of the tower, you can nail the bottom frame in place with one nail in each corner. Square that end of the box or tower as you do the nailing.

Tie the tower to a tree or fence post so it won't blow over in a strong wind.

After living in the tower for two weeks or more, released birds will recall to those left inside.

Paint the tower, tie or chain it to a fence post or tree trunk for support, place bricks or treated wood blocks under it to help avoid rot, and put your quail inside. After two weeks, you can begin releasing a few birds and recalling them every day. Do this for several days before working dogs with the freed birds.

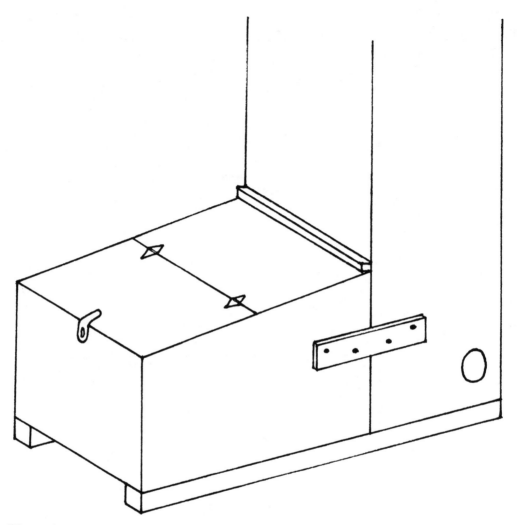

Dimensions are unimportant, but build the sidecar with a sloped roof. Fasten a 2-by-2 to the tower to keep weather out when the sidecar slides into place beneath it.

The sidecar addition, if needed, can be built according to the drawing. When installing, remove the access door from the tower so the birds can pass through the opening to get food and water. Two boards attach the addition to the tower. Bolt them to the tower first, then reach through the new entrance door to bolt the boards to the addition.

Step 16

Instant Steady to Wing and Shot

There's a lot of controversy about whether bird dogs should be steady to wing, steady to wing and shot, or not steady at all. Steady, of course, means continuing to stand at the point site. Steady to wing is standing as the birds fly. Steady to shot is standing until after the shot and until ordered to FETCH.

Horseback field-trailers insist that their dogs be steady to both wing and shot. Some excellent hunters do, too, reasoning that a running dog can't mark a falling bird as accurately as can a stationary dog. You can easily prove this for yourself. Have someone throw a ball into weeds as you run. Find it. Do the same thing when you're standing still. Easier? Sure.

In addition, a dog racing away at the flush may not even see a bird drop. If the covey fans, the dog could be chasing in a direction quite different from that in which you're shooting.

Another concern is that not all birds may be in the air with the first flush. If there are laggards still on the ground, the unsteady dog will probably flush them; these birds could have provided extra shooting had the dog been steady.

An unsteady pheasant dog that can't be stopped from chasing after the flush may get you banned from future hunts. An illegal hen gets up, so nobody shoots. Your dog doesn't know the difference, though, so he chases the hen down the cornfield, flushing legal roosters left and right—all, of course, out of shotgun range.

Some hunters agree that dogs should be steady to wing, but want their dogs on the way to a retrieve when the shotgun fires. Small delays can permit cripples to escape. These sportsmen don't care that a few laggard quail may be accidentally flushed after the gun is empty. It's the bird they shot that they want in the bag.

As practical as some degree of steady sounds, most hunters don't demand it. In fact, when hunters acquire professionally trained dogs that are steady to wing and shot, those dogs are rarely steady in any way by the end of the season.

The dog doesn't *want* to be steady because of the way most training is conducted. It's a restriction of the dog's natural hunting urges. The pros call the process, "breaking." The dog's instincts are to hesitate on point long enough to accurately locate the prey, then jump in for the kill. The farther we get from his natural behavior, the harder it is to train and keep the dog trained.

On top of that, hunters don't provide very good examples. The dog sees you break and run to catch a cripple. He sees you break and run to get a better shot. Guess who follows your example! Of course. There went all the training that you or a pro put into steadying the dog. It sometimes becomes awkward, even when you hope to enforce steadiness. By the time you realize that the dog broke and ran, he might be picking up your dead bird. Can you scream at him while he delivers a quail to your hand? Hardly. He'd stop doing that, too.

My father was like the vast majority of hunters. He didn't care that his dogs weren't steady. In fact, his dogs broke point *before* the flush because he ordered them to do the flushing on command. He wanted to be ready and positioned for the shot, not standing with one foot in the air, or straddling a fence, when the birds flew. Yes, sometimes Dad's dogs were looking in the wrong direction when the bird went down, but Dad never was. He could mark the fall almost as he shot, and swing to repeat it on another bird. If his dog didn't mark, Dad didn't mind playing escort to the vicinity of the fall. With that much help, the dog could use his nose to do the rest.

My guess is that at this point you don't know which you'd rather have your dog do—flush on command, steady to wing, or steady to wing and shot. If you reread this, searching for a clue of what I think is best, I doubt that you'd find it. There are situations when each has advantages over the others. I have good news for you, though, especially if you started Buckshot as a puppy. You have a steady to wing and shot dog that flushes on command. You have it all, and it comes almost automatically because you started right.

It was natural for little Buckshot to want to break point and try to catch the pigeon, so we used a behavioral trick to lengthen his points. We ordered him to flush the bird before he got the urge himself. Then gradually, bird after bird, he became accustomed to accepting the order as the time to go. We began increasing the length of each point. Finally, Buckshot would hold his point almost indefinitely while waiting for the command.

Now we can take advantage of that same canine behavioral trait to provide a steady dog in an instant. You see, dogs are highly opposed to being restrained from doing what their nature suggests is right. When "broken" to doing it our way, they look for loopholes to get around it. That turns steadying into a lifelong training problem for some dogs. Dogs are not opposed to waiting a few moments to carry out their natural urges. If we say no, yes is on their minds. If we're saying in effect, not right now, but in a minute, they're content to wait.

See the connection? Buckshot already flushes on command. If you withheld that command, he's steady. He doesn't go.

Obviously, you can't pull this off every time or it won't work very long. Be slick about it, especially at first. As you move up to flush the bird yourself, cut a wide circle around the dog. Don't allow your motion to urge him to follow. Add a verbal WHOA and hand signal for reinforcement as you walk forward. Say ALL RIGHT as the birds flush and your gun comes up. All you've done is delay Buckshot's break. Repeat this perhaps once every three or four birds, so your dog isn't sure when he'll go, but doesn't suspect that he'll never get to go.

When that's working well, withhold your ALL RIGHT command until you've shot. Again, do this only once every three or four birds. After that, mix it up. Delay sending him more and more often. Eventually, you'll be able to fetch the bird yourself, if you like, while the dog waits because he knows that his turn will come. In fact, trainers keep dogs steady by occasionally fetching the bird themselves. The dog doesn't break because he's not sure it's his turn.

Those who didn't start their pups young can teach their dog to flush on command now. Buckshot already knows ALL RIGHT from being released in the field. It means go on, do what you want, you're released. When he points, use the WHOA whistle, if necessary, so he holds his point until you arrive. Get ready to shoot, and give the command. If your dog doesn't make the connection, walk up beside him. As you give the command this time, step forward with the leg that's closest to your dog's eye. He'll go with the motion. After a few times, he'll understand without you having to move.

The ALL RIGHT command also lets you quietly release the dog from point to move up on birds that are running. It's much handier and quicker than walking up to tap the dog on the head as field-trialers do. You can also remain outside the taller cover for a more open shot when the time comes.

If your dog wasn't started as a puppy and is having trouble being steady to wing and shot, return to the steel drum and fly birds, instead of paper plates, after the WHOA command.

Training does not always go as smoothly as it might with those dogs that weren't started before 16 weeks old. If your dog just can't grasp the idea of standing steady to wing and shot while awaiting the release order, then return to the steel drum. When the wind is right, plant a bird behind a clump or pile of weeds. Command WHOA as you lift the dog onto the drum. The scent coming from the bird will stiffen the WHOA into a point. Now reach into your bag or bird vest and throw a pigeon across the dog's line of vision. The hidden bird remains undisturbed because its scent adds one more reason why the dog should remain standing instead of breaking. When three or four birds are released (enough for one session), carry your dog from the barrel and away from the hidden bird to help ingrain the idea that he should never voluntarily leave a live bird.

After he's standing to flush without breaking, begin firing your shotgun into the air after tossing each bird.

When very reliable on both wing and shot, repeat the exercises beside the drum.

A hog-wire-mesh fence is excellent to enforce steady to wing and shot.

After that, look for a hog-wire-mesh fence that the dog can't get through. If none is available buy a 20 or 30-foot length of mesh. It can be tied to a barbed-wire fence. Check the wind so it will blow bird scent from a launcher through the fence to the dog. When Buckshot points, add WHOA, and flush the bird. If he breaks, the fence stops him from getting to the bird, but you have more work to do on WHOA and on the drum. Obviously, if he breaks, don't shoot the bird. In fact, never shoot a bird that your dog flushes before the command. It's hard to get hunting buddies to go along with this, but if they don't, hunt by yourself during at least the dog's first season.

If Buckshot does remain steady when the bird is flushed behind the fence, shoot the bird. If he's steady to shot, release him to make the fetch. If not, the fence again prevents him from getting to the bird. Those dogs that recognize it's possible to go around the fence will require a check cord. I have a wire-mesh exercise pen, so I can plant a bird outside, free a dog inside, and have him find and point it regardless of wind direction. He can never get to the bird until I release him by verbal command and open the gate, or lift him over the fence, whichever seems appropriate at the time.

Scott's hobbles may help gain compliance from a dog determined to break on wing or shot.

Those of you who are having serious trouble keeping your dog steady, but who are determined to do so, might consider the hobbles invented by Tom Scott. (See appendix for address.) Nylon-web anklets are attached above three of the dog's feet with Velcro. When the dog points, you approach, and snap a connector to D-rings on all three anklets. If the dog breaks at wing or shot, he yanks his own feet right out from under himself. If he doesn't break, unsnap the connector and let him fetch. With practice, he learns that remaining steady is the wise choice.

Consider, also, that maturity rates vary widely among breeds as well as individuals. If you bought a submissive pup that pointed at eight weeks, he'll steady early. Dominant pups think of carrying out their own ideas, and they are slow about accepting yours. Unless your dog is actively searching for game when in the field, holds his points for at least a minute, and obeys the WHOA command, he's not ready to be steadied. Some intelligent, submissive dogs learn it before a year. Others are 2 or 3 years or older before they accept breaking to wing and shot. This can be vastly accelerated by our method of starting with the right pup, teaching him to flush on command, and advancing from there at the rate he can accept without being pressured. If you didn't start early on this pup, resolve to do so with the next.

Step 17

Range and Search Control

Control of their dog's range is a major concern in the minds of a great many hunters and amateur trainers. And it *is* mostly in their minds; they fear that their dog will "run away." It does happen on rare occasions, but won't if you train according to the instructions in this book.

Trainers call the problem "bolting." The dog vanishes like a streak when released and doesn't return until exhausted. It happened far more often in the old days than it does now. I saw a classic example with an English setter belonging to a couple who were obedience-class trainers. The pressure they exerted on that dog to make him obey was extreme. The woman, especially, related to the dog only in screaming commands. Simply put, the dog couldn't stand to be around its owners, and at every opportunity, it escaped to enjoy the world alone and away from the abuse. Most of today's trainers are much more sensible and far more kind. Their dogs, especially those less than 3 years old, will make some pretty wide runs when first released. After all, they've been restrained in a kennel. They're running off a bit of exuberance, but they'll soon settle down.

A more important fact about a dog's range that most amateurs don't understand is that it's inherited. Your dog came into this world with a ready-made idea of how far to the front he should search. That's why it's so important to select the right pup from the right parents. Horseback field-trialers say only about 5 percent of their pointers and English setters are capable of ranging from horizon to horizon. A hunter on foot, however, with a dog that makes casts of one-half-mile or more, is helplessly out of control most of the time. The same breeds of pointers and setters from Shoot-to-Retrieve trials run at close range because that's one of the characteristics the breeders select for. An English setter from grouse-hunting stock will quarter better at a much closer range. They're selected to run within hearing range of the dog bell or beeper collar. When you have the wrong dog for the way you hunt, in the type of cover you hunt, you're fighting the genes. It's like trying to pull a green limb down to grow in a lower position. As soon as you let go, it springs back to the way nature planned it.

All is not lost, however. There are things you can do to maintain the pull on that "limb" and make it grow at least partly in the direction you prefer. The first of those things is whistle control, and you've already taught that. You won't enjoy having to hack your dog back continually, but at least you'll have the ability to turn your dog before he gets too far out.

Dog-supply catalogs sell a pair of balls on cords that attach to the collar and slap back and forth on the dog's front legs. The harder the dogs run, the harder the balls slap, so they do slow down some excessively wide-running dogs. More incorrigible dogs run with chains hanging from their collars. A sack with a few rocks can be tied to the collar with a rope and dragged by the dog during his training runs. The weight can be adjusted to the dog's requirements. If the dog can be kept in range while training, it is hoped that he will get the idea that birds are found, and from his viewpoint "caught," only when he's searching near you.

For that reason, it's also best to train for range control in an area that has no birds except those you provide. If the dog knows wild birds are out there, he'll extend his range farther and farther to find them.

Whenever practicing, always run the dog into the wind. Whenever possible, do the same thing later when hunting. Obviously, dogs' ability to scent birds is much enhanced by running into the wind. Wind direction, however, influences running patterns as well. Dogs quarter into the wind, so they range closer. Running downwind, they cast much farther, often in straight lines. They may then quarter back into the wind, run wide to one side or the other, or perhaps even swing behind you. Make good, close quartering search patterns more of a habit by always running into the wind.

Make it very pleasant for the dog to be near you, too. If he's running too wide, don't grumble about it every time he does swing past near you. Instead, say "There's my pretty dog! Good boy!" You sound happy, so he feels happy. Maybe he'll swing past more often and make both of you happy. Always touch him when he swings past close enough.

Wide runners heat up rapidly, of course. So carry a clean bottle of water.

The size depends upon the length of the session. While hunting, you may need a two-liter soda bottle. When you see Buckshot panting hard, whistle him in and pour some water in his mouth. Go slowly until he learns how to drink it this way. After he realizes you always have water, he has one more strong reason to stay near you.

An old stunt that works for awhile is hiding. When the dog reaches too far, stand behind a tree or bush. When he does swing back, you're not where he thought you should be. You'll see him look around in a panic, thinking he's lost. Make him find you. He'll be more careful about running off and risking this again. When he does locate you, be happy about it. "There you are! Good boy!"

Don't depend on the hiding trick alone, however. Once your dog learns the territory and/or gains confidence in himself, it no longer works very well.

When hunters have range control problems, it's almost always with a running pattern that's too big. The opposite can happen as well, however, and it's even more aggravating. The disinterest of a "boot polisher" just going along for the walk is harder to deal with than the over-interest of a hard-going wide ranger. Exuberance can be tamed somewhat; simply aging helps. But trying to motivate a lackadaisical, indifferent loafer may be impossible. Your only hope is to awaken a latent interest in birds by putting him in an enclosure with a pigeon and by letting him chase birds tossed under his nose.

Fortunately, not all short-ranging dogs lack bird interest. Some simply are not independent enough to reach out as far as you think they should. Nevertheless they may hunt their limited range in a very animated fashion. These dogs can be drawn out a bit just as wide rangers can be drawn in somewhat.

You've already taught ALL RIGHT as a signal to leave your side, or go on. For the short ranger, start preceding the ALL RIGHT command with two quick toots on the whistle. When he understands the new whistle command, you can use it to push him forward when necessary.

This is also a handy command in case a less-than-animated short ranger starts pottering on foot scent. It's OK to follow foot scent at a quick pace, but studying foot scent is a waste of time. Walk up to crowd him. Whistle him to move on. Some trainers add emphasis to the whistle with a marble to the butt from a slingshot.

I had a short-ranging Brittany that wanted to double-check everything. He'd smell something, move on a couple steps, then return as if undecided and sniff again. Crowding, the whistle, and a few pops on the rear cured most of it.

Habitual false pointing is a behavior that has to be handled differently. I bring this up here because if your dog is doing it, you might consider moving him on in the same manner as a potterer. Don't risk punishment with a marble, however, when the dog thinks he's pointing birds. Cure it by indifference. Kick cover for the birds. If they aren't there, just walk off. With experience, the young dog will become more careful about what kind of scent he points.

Don't confuse habitual false pointing with the occasional false point that happens to nearly all dogs, however. Conditions might cause scent to smell stronger that day. Maybe the bird flew just before you got there.

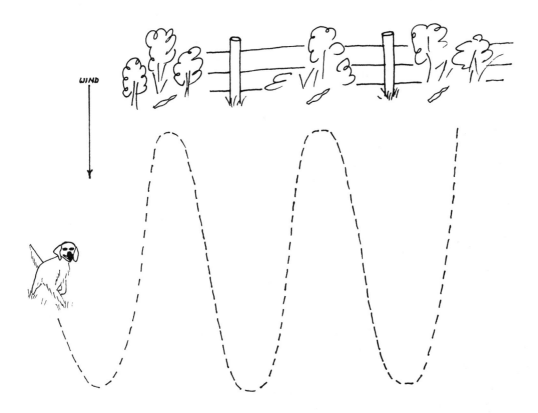

A search system can help you either draw your dog in or push him out. Suppose the wind is from the west, and you have a north–south fencerow as shown in the drawing. Plant three birds about 70 yards apart along the fence in an otherwise birdless area. Bring the dog across the fence, also from the west, and start him moving downwind. That's contrary to normal searching practice, but it will probably send Buckshot on a long downwind run. Don't follow him. Walk about 60 yards beyond the fence yourself, then turn and walk parallel to the fence until you're almost directly downwind from the first bird.

By now, your dog has made his long run and is headed back. If not, wait for a moment when he's not greatly interested in something, then whistle him back. His run was unproductive, but soon after he swings past you traveling into the wind, he'll catch scent. You'll see him start acting birdy. If you have a hawk whistle, blow it. With repetition, he'll associate the whistle with birds, and become more cautious. Later, it can become the signal to hunt closer.

After flushing and shooting this bird, walk downwind again. When Buckshot makes his wide run, turn and repeat the whole maneuver on the second bird, and then on the third.

Do this two or three times a week, if you can. Vary the locations so he doesn't start running a paper route. If you have an intelligent dog, he'll realize that every time he found a bird he was 60 or 70 yards from you. Maybe the secret to finding birds without a lot of wasted effort is to search near you. If you can repeat this often enough, his shorter range pattern will become habitual. You'll notice an improved response to the turn whistle as well. He'll come to understand that sometimes there are birds when you whistle him around and he'll be anxious to check it out.

Under actual circumstances with fewer birds and longer spaces in between, the dog may sometimes lapse into wide ranging, but you can whistle him back, then hold him with the hawk whistle. Use the hawk whistle only when you're into good cover and are pretty sure that birds are in the vicinity. Fooling the dog too often will undo his training.

The short ranging dog also can be trained on the setup in the drawing. In this case, simply walk along the downwind side of the fencerow. In the beginning, you may have to get him within 20 yards, or whatever his range is, before he finds the birds. Don't worry. Next time, plant the birds in exactly the same place. He'll remember, and very soon he'll be racing ahead of you to find the next bird. After he's doing that, vary locations so he has to search harder, but keep the birds about as far apart as you want the dog to range. If repeated often enough, your preferred range becomes habitual.

An extra thought: Some quartering dogs, especially youngsters, swing behind you as they come across. Field-trial judges hate this because it's a waste of time. It's not of tremendous importance to hunters, however, especially when we understand why dogs do it. It's a gesture of politeness. The alpha wolf hunts to the front. Crossing in front, therefore, is a challenge to leadership in canine language. Your intelligently submissive yearling may not be ready to try that. Don't worry about it. The birds will eventually draw him out, and your dog will come to understand that it's OK to cross to the front.

Step 18

Adjusting Cover Search to Bird Species

Trying to make round pegs fit in square holes is a practice more widespread among bird-dog enthusiasts than in any other canine endeavor. That's because there are more choices and, therefore, more chances to mismatch dog and bird. The birds, themselves, vary widely in behavior patterns. Around much of the world, bird dogs have been developed to best handle the particular behavior patterns of local birds. Whims of breeders also become a factor. Field-trial fads add another dimension. In the worst scenario, the hunter buys a big running pointer, reads a book by a fellow who trains bobwhite-quail dogs, then tries to train his dog to hunt pheasants or grouse.

Adding to the dilemma is the way most of us choose dogs. For many of us, first priority is *looks.* If it looks like the grand dog Uncle Joe had, if it's the same color as Dad's good ol' Red, or if it resembles the hero dog in an impressive magazine article, then never mind that he's bred for a different purpose. Surely, he'll be a great hunter if his hair is the right length or if the spots are in the right places.

Sight, however, is our primary sense. If dogs were breeding humans, we wouldn't be selected for what's between the ears, either. It would be the odor under the arms that would count!

Until we develop a system to match hunter and dog (breed as well as individual canine) in a logical, efficient manner, we can only match training with teaching the dog where his prey will be found. After that come certain bird handling traits that should be enhanced, or perhaps looked for in the next dog, if they can't be developed in this one.

Because of where and how bobwhite quail live, it doesn't make sense to drill quartering into the dog. It's better if he hunts "objectives," for example briar patches, fencerows, stream bank, wood edges, or dense cover edges. Quartering larger expanses of bare fields or searching deep into fields of heavy cover are wastes of time. Quail are careful about getting caught in cover so thick that it's hard to make an escape, and they don't venture far into the open unless it's the only place to find food.

Quail spend the night as well as their midday rest period in protective, but not very dense, cover. This could be briars, up a small draw or branch, under brush at the edge of woods, or in such places as thin weeds grown up through branches of a fallen tree. During feeding hours, they'll be where the grain is, but only as far into open fields as is necessary to find food. To predict where they are, look for grain fields, find suitable nearby protective cover, then figure out the safe route of travel between the two. A route that can be traveled unseen might be a fencerow, finger of woods, grassy drainage out of a field, or a brush-and/or-tree-lined stream cutting through a field. When no such path exists, look for protective cover adjacent to fields. Quail will be feeding as near as possible to protective cover or routes and will be in that protection when resting.

Knowing this, it makes sense to arrange for the quail-dog trainee to find his birds (planted, recall, or released) in these same kinds of areas he will later be expected to search. Dogs remember where they were successful, and the intelligent dogs become wise in searching out similar areas wherever they hunt. It also makes sense to position training birds in a manner appropriate to the time of day, because some dogs become wise to this as well. While the quail dog can range far and wide in relatively open feeding areas, and when searching distant objectives such as possible travel routes, it's best to encourage him to hunt at close range when in and/or near resting cover.

Western quail are quite different. The Mearns quail, a relatively rare bird found in a small area of the Southwest, holds as well as the bobwhite. A wide-ranging dog, as long as he holds his points well, would seem suitable for this species, and can be at times. In practice, however, the close ranger is more productive because he isn't so often out of sight behind the next ridge in the mountainous country Mearns quail prefer. All other Western quail are inclined to run out from under a dog's point.

The blue scaled quail of the Southwest is justifiably nicknamed "blue racer." This is far and away the worst of the runners, and yet these birds will hold at times. If the cover is adequate, the covey will hold. In general, scaled quail hold much better as singles after the covey is broken.

Gambel quail are runners, but they're no match for scaled quail. The same can be said for California (or valley) quail, as well as mountain quail. Mountain quail whistle to regroup very soon after a covey-break, so you can sometimes guide your dog to the singles.

In all cases, a really fast, snappy dog can pin Western quail by showing up so rapidly and suddenly that the birds opt for hiding instead of risking flight. I watched a Texas pointer jet past me so fast that only someone who knew him would suspect that he had anything on his mind besides racing the wind. He sailed off a drywash bank, hit the middle just once, and smelled birds in midair a split second before landing on the opposite bank. I saw him stiffen and come on point while still in the air, and he hit the ground like a statue. Engineers should study that dog to reinvent automobile brakes. The scaled quail held like bobwhites.

Dogs like that, with noses as fast as their high-powered legs, are rare, however. Average dogs are too slow to get the advantage of surprise, so the quail run. One Texas hunter solved the problem by switching from bird dogs to a border collie that ran ahead, circled and herded the scaled quail back toward him. Some bird dogs become smart enough through experience to circle birds. If you are persistent, circling can be taught to a very intelligent dog.

Leon Measures taught two pointers to work as a team. Day after day, he led one dog around in a circle to back the other from the opposite side of a planted bird. Eventually, it became habitual, and the second dog would circle on his own to back from the opposite side. After three months, it clicked in these dogs' heads that this is the way to pin scaled quail.

Without doubt, the circling dog is the best for all Western quail except the Mearns. A single dog with this learned trait can move the birds toward you if he's also very careful not to crowd them into flight. When the birds realize they're caught between you to the front, and the dog to the rear, they usually stop and hold to point.

Opening-day pheasants may hold to point, but after the slightest education they learn to run as well as Western quail. Again, a fast, snappy approach is the way to pin pheasants, but too few dogs combine that trait with adequate nose and bird sense. Like the Western-quail dogs, the best of those dogs that don't have a snappy approach are those that learn to circle.

Although less effective, the other choice is to teach a slower dog to lock on point the instant it catches a whiff of body scent. If the pheasant runs, the dog trails cautiously to avoid a flush, halting to point whenever the bird stops. If the dog fails to grasp this naturally, he can be taught to hold point until you arrive, even if the bird leaves. After you catch up, you release him with the ALL RIGHT command to resume trailing. Occasionally, you catch up. At least as often, the trail grows cold and is lost because you can't move along fast enough. Don't let the pheasant dog develop the habit of pottering on a bird's foot scent because he'll never catch up with his birds.

Some Western-quail dogs hunt in this same manner. In practice, they more often function as flushing than pointing dogs, because few hunters will refuse to shoot either accidentally flushed pheasants or Western quail. If this same dog also will be used on birds that do hold, it's wise to teach stop-to-flush. Otherwise, the dog may become an oversize spaniel instead of a pointing dog. Whether you shoot birds accidentally flushed or insist on stop-to-flush, the unpredictable nature of the pheasant demands a close-ranging dog.

When training a pheasant dog, plant your birds where pheasants are found: in corn and sorghum fields, fencerows, or in reasonably heavy cover near these areas. Don't fail to train in marshy spots. This comes as a surprise to many hunters because these aren't water birds, but pheasants do like to sneak off and hide in the cattails and other aquatic weeds. It doesn't have to be a big marsh. In arid country, a little wet spot set low in an otherwise dry drainage will attract pheasants. Teach the pheasant dog to be superb at quartering if you hunt in grain fields.

Grouse and woodcock hunting also requires dogs that quarter well. After the dog learns quartering, do bird training in the woods. That's where grouse are found, of course, but there's a second reason. The dog can't see you as readily in the woods, so he doesn't range as far. Training in the woods is a good tactic for shortening range on other types of bird dogs, too. For forest grouse (ruffed, blue, or spruce) it's essential that the dog range within hearing of his bell or beeper.

You can't raise grouse and woodcock to train dogs, but pigeons, followed later by quail, work well as starters. Grouse like logging roads, especially those near water. Plant your training birds near the edges of roads and as much as 50 yards back into the woods.

While the fast, snappy performer works best on most birds, only an extremely sudden appearance will make a grouse hold to point. More often, caution works better. The grouse dog should hunt in an animated fashion, rather than plodding. The first criteria of a good grouse dog, however, is that he lock down at the first sniff of bird.

Woodcocks hold well, so most bird dogs find them easy to handle. They're found in woodsy lowlands, so a close-ranging dog that can be seen or heard is essential. Train with birds in the muddy, marshy areas where woodcocks will be digging worms when the season opens in the fall. Woodcock dogs must be good retrievers because human eyes won't see many of these well camouflaged birds after they've fallen on dead leaves.

Prairie grouse (sharptails, sage grouse, and prairie chickens) don't consistently hold to point. The young and/or ignorant birds may, but they're unpredictable. Educated prairie grouse are very spooky, and their education may not require human teachers. Already pursued by coyotes, they may be preconditioned to fear dogs. As with other grouse dogs, a dog that locks into point at the first whiff will have the best chance of holding prairie grouse until you arrive. And you shouldn't be far away because the effective dog is working near you.

Step 19

Backing

Hunting with buddies who also own dogs requires minimum standards of polite manners. If your dog is steady to wing and shot, and his isn't, yours won't be for very long either. The only solutions are hunting his dog today and yours the next time, or hunting so far apart that the dogs are never hunting together. Whether a dog is steady or not, however, depends greatly on personal opinion, willingness to train, what the owner does with his dog in competition, and so on.

Backing, however, goes beyond mannerly behavior. A dog that won't back can destroy a hunt—never mind what he does to himself in field trials. When a dog won't back, he's usually jealous of the other dog's bird find. So he runs past the pointing dog to steal the find. Pretty soon, both dogs are crowding forward to steal the points, and the birds are flushed before the hunters arrive. It can get so competitive that both dogs are racing each other to flush the birds. In one day, many months of training can go down the drain.

The most simple way to teach backing is with another dog that holds his points well. Plant a bird, get the other dog on point, and bring the trainee in on check cord. Try to arrange it so you suddenly come upon the training dog. Maybe he's just over the crest of a hill, or maybe you're bringing the trainee along the edge of a thick woods, and the pointing dog is just around the corner.

It's best if the wind direction permits the trainee to whiff the bird at about the same instant he sees the other dog on point. If luck is with you, your dog will smell the bird, lock down, hold his point, and begin to recognize that whether he smells the bird or not, he should stop when another dog is pointing. Some dogs catch on instantly and are natural backers from the start.

A dominant dog, though, may have trouble being number two. In that case, you have the check cord. WHOA him the instant he sees the other dog pointing. If he tries to creep, pick him up and return him to the spot with another WHOA. If he breaks, do an about-face for better leverage when he hits the end of the check cord. Again, return him bodily. Slap the front of his chest to reinforce another WHOA command. Next time, use a choke chain to apply more pressure to his unmannerly ways.

A ground cable is great for teaching dogs to back. Tom Scott shows how he does it right next to a traveled road.

Those trainers who have set up a ground cable can use it to teach backing. The end in use depends upon wind direction. The pointing dog is off cable and well beyond the end. The trainee is attached to the runner cable. When he sees the other dog pointing, he either stops and backs before getting to the end of the cable, or the stake dumps him. When he becomes wise to where the cable ends, drive a staple stake over the cable to force stops in new locations.

It is best if the cable has a 90-degree turn around a building or fence, so the trainee suddenly comes upon the pointing dog. It's also best if the wind direction is such that it delivers bird scent at about the same time he sees the pointing dog.

Use plenty of scent at first. Plant a crate of pigeons or quail instead of one bird. Place a wet towel under the crate to enhance the scent. If the temperature is cold, use a hot towel for even greater enhancement.

If it is inconvenient or impossible for you to train with another dog, you can use a phony. My most dramatic experience was with a fiberglass statue Tom Scott had an artist sculpt of his dog Speck. I was walking alongside a building toward a kennel with a borrowed dog I was returning. Neither I nor the dog knew the statue was just around the corner at the end of the building. It came into view suddenly, and we both saw it at the same moment. I recognized what it was and walked a few more steps before I realized the dog was no longer with me. I looked back to see a dog with mediocre pointing instincts locked up like the Statue of Liberty. The worried expression on this dog's face made me realize that whether it's a statue or a silhouette, the dog perceived it as real. It appears to be pointing, which another pointing dog should understand and respect. What the dog also greatly respects, however, is that this steady, staring, motionless stance is unmistakably threatening. It might be threatening to him! To bolt would invite chase and attack, so he, too, stands motionless until further notice.

I carried that dog away to reinforce the idea that he should never voluntarily break a backing point. After a few encounters, I'm sure the dog's fear of a statue subsides, but by then backing is becoming a habit.

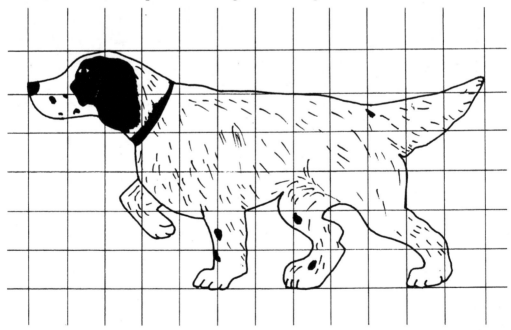

I found this ol' Phony-Point, the best I've seen, in Tony Zupcic's yard. By enlarging these squares to four by four inches and drawing the appropriate lines in each square on a sheet of three-quarter-inch plywood, you can reproduce and use this canine silhouette to teach your dog to back.

I have included a drawing of ol' Phony-Point that you can reproduce on three-quarter-inch plywood and cut out with a saber saw. Paint it white with black spots, and bolt stakes to the legs. Plant it in the same types of locations described earlier for teaching backing with a live dog on point.

A silhouette called The Back Off – By Jack is also available – so you don't have to build one – in supply catalogs or from the manufacturer. (See appendix for address.) The phony is also available with a spring-loaded device that flips the silhouette suddenly and noisily upright, which provides a marvelous surprise factor.

Step 20

Must Heel

The obedience lessons in this and the next three steps are optional and do not necessarily precede the force-fetch. I include them here for those of you who think your dog could use the extra discipline and control as well as for those who want to make their dogs into better citizens.

Your dog was introduced to HEEL during WHOA training, so maybe he already knows it well enough to suit you. Maybe you prefer to use a leash instead of HEEL, anyway. That's OK. While it's handier and prettier to walk out of the field with a dog at HEEL, I'd just as soon he'd be dragging a leash as well. It's a reminder to the dog and something I can step on or quickly grab in an emergency.

You may question why I waited so long to explain *must* HEEL. Why wasn't it taught way back there with WHOA? When taught together the two commands inhibit some dogs and they think they should stay at your side even in the field. It could have stalled progress, and it might have diminished some of your dog's dash and animation. By now, the use of ALL RIGHT to send him on, plus extensive time in the field, will make this unlikely. If it occurs somewhat at this time, ignore it. He'll get over it quickly because we've given priority to fun in the field.

224

Must HEEL, coming behind a good introduction, is almost instantly understood by dogs. They already know what they should do. When they choose not to obey, they cause their own discomfort. The fact that they grasp it quickly does not mean that they learn it permanently, however. It has to be practiced. Heeling the dog to and from training and to and from the vehicle will probably keep it adequately etched in his mind.

To teach *must* HEEL, give the command, stride forward, and allow the check cord to slide freely through your hand when the dog decides to range forward.

To begin, use a check cord and the dog's ordinary collar. Don't do this exercise on the ground cable because you'll need to unpredictably change directions. Pull Buckshot into position near your leg as you say HEEL and stride forward. With no more HEEL training than this youngster has had, odds are that he'll ignore the command enough to surge forward instead of walking by your side. Let the check cord slide freely through your hand so he feels no resistance to his movement.

With the dog well to the front, do an abrupt about-face. You may have to keep an eye on Buckshot with your peripheral vision, but do not make eye contact with the dog.

When your dog gets 10 or 20 feet ahead, throw extra slack into the check cord, grip the cord firmly, and do a sudden about-face. Just hitting the end of the cord would be a shock to the dog, but the added force of you moving in the opposite direction is a jolting surprise that may flip him end for end.

Very quickly, an intelligent dog will learn to outsmart this discomfort by staying close to your side and keeping an eye on your changes of direction.

Read carefully; *this is important.* The first thing the dog will do as he flips is look at you. He knows you gave the command that he ignored and he suspects you were somehow responsible for his unhappy experience, even though he left you some distance behind. *If he makes eye contact with you in that crucial moment, he will know you did it, and nothing will be gained from the lesson.* While he'll understand that you don't want him to disobey HEEL, he'll still want to disobey HEEL, and he will.

On the other hand, if he does not make eye contact with you, he isn't sure what or who was responsible for his flip. You were already walking away, not even noticing, so surely it wasn't you. He'll run to catch up. As he does, pull him into position as you again command HEEL.

It will be an amazingly intelligent dog that won't immediately, or very soon, run ahead a second time. Repeat the whole performance. *Remember: No eye contact.*

By the third such experience, submissively intelligent dogs begin putting it together. You said HEEL. Instead, he ran ahead and didn't keep an eye on you. You changed direction, and the results were distinctly uncomfortable! Maybe he could outsmart this dilemma by staying close and keeping an eye on your direction changes. He may even do this through several of your sudden changes of route.

You can be sure, however, that this isn't the end of it. He'll forget. Or he'll have to test it one more time to be sure. It depends on the individual. Dominant males may try again and again. If your dog makes a habit of avoiding eye contact when you give an order, he doesn't want to hear it. Worse he thinks if he doesn't listen, he won't have to obey. He'll test it repeatedly. Put a choke chain on him for a better awakening.

In minutes, most dogs will be walking at your side without restraint, but they'll forget the lesson if you don't continue to practice.

The average dog will walk obediently next to you after no more than a couple minutes of *must* HEEL training. Praise him and stop the lesson for today.

After he has thought about it for about 24 hours, try him again. Do this every day until he will HEEL by your side on command through changes of speed as well as direction. Sometimes rushing forward will tempt him to race you, and out front he goes. Fine. It's an opportunity for another reinforcement of the lesson. If he's too smart for that, HEEL him past something more tempting like another dog (or the neighbor's cat). Until he continues to HEEL—even when tempted—*must* HEEL is not completely learned. Even then, HEEL will have to be practiced, or the dog won't "stay learned."

Going through this training experience won't change the dog's personality, however. It will make him HEEL somewhere near your leg, but his natural urges will continue to manifest themselves. The dominant dog still wants to surge ahead. He may not be far enough ahead to let you escape his peripheral vision, but you may consider this distance too far for proper control. When he's ahead, it's disobedience waiting to happen. He can also be in your way. Suppose you're about to step on a rattlesnake and need to make a quick left turn. That's no time to stumble over his rear end.

A leafy limb helps keep the pupil reminded of where you want him to HEEL.

With sufficient practice, and several props, the dominant dog can be made to HEEL where you want. Yank off a leafy limb as you HEEL away from the field. If he tries to surge forward, swat his nose. The swishing leaves add a threatening sound, so it's more convincing than a simple switch.

Practice HEEL beside a fence, and crowd the dog that always tries to surge ahead.

Also try heeling the dog between you and a fence. The instant he tries to move ahead, cut him off with your left leg. He may try to duck around to your right to surge forward, but keeping the leash or check cord across your front will stop that move.

For the dominant dog that surges ahead, HEEL in a counterclockwise circle so you're frequently rapping his head with your knee.

For backyard HEEL practice, walk the dominant dog in a counterclockwise circle. (If you shoot left-handed, and prefer the dog to HEEL on your right, do the opposite, of course.) When he tries to surge forward, he'll tangle with your legs. Don't make it a gentle collision.

The submissive dog, if you don't want him to hang back, may have to be heeled in a clockwise circle so he's always having to catch up.

The submissive dog usually isn't a problem on HEEL, at least not for hunters. Those training to obedience-competition standards may find this dog hanging back too far. HEEL this dog in a clockwise circle so he's always hurrying to catch up. With enough practice, he'll stay in position.

A length of electrical conduit with a snap in the end will help keep the dog from heeling too close or too far from your leg.

Other problems sometimes encountered are heeling too far away, or too close to your leg. You don't want Buckshot bumping your leg every few steps. Nor do you want him moving so far out that he tries to slip beyond control. Bolt a snap in the end of a length of electrical conduit. Use a piece of rigid water pipe if your dog is big and strong enough to bend conduit. Snap the pipe to his collar, decide what distance is comfortable for you, and with a firm grip on the pipe, force him to walk right there. With enough practice (a few minutes daily for as long as six weeks for some dogs) he'll get it right.

Caution: Dogs are wild when taken from the kennel. It's tempting to "run the edge off him" before obedience lessons. Some trainers even recommend it. Don't do it. This sets up a pattern of wild behavior every time you let him out to train or hunt. Insist that the dog HEEL from the moment he comes out of the gate and until released to do something else. A hunting dog must always be obedient.

Step 21

Sit and Sit-Come

SIT is not a popular command among bird-dog trainers. Most believe it will, sooner or later, result in the dog sitting in the presence of birds. When this happens, however, it's usually with planted birds, and the dog has learned it's a game. Chances are, the trainer is trying to lengthen the dog's point, or is wasting time in some other way—or so the dog thinks—so he sits down to wait the boss out in greater comfort. Few dogs, whether taught SIT or not, actually park their butts when in the exciting presence of wild birds.

Another thing to consider is that a few dogs would sit in the presence of planted birds, even if they never heard the SIT command. Most bird dogs find it more comfortable to sit. A few of you discovered that during WHOA training. WHOA is a command that says, "Don't just do something, stand there," and the dog figures why stand when he can sit.

There are many occasions at home and in the vehicle when the dog should sit patiently on command. It may simply stop him from being a pest—or being able to sit him on the floorboards may save someone's car seat from mud or toenail tears. Don't be afraid to add SIT to Buckshot's citizenship credentials.

I find that SIT is important for the dog that's having trouble with the COME command. As I've said before, I don't like teaching a WHOA-COME sequence because it teaches the dog to be anxious to break while he's on WHOA. I prefer the WHOA-HEEL sequence. You can, however, use a SIT-COME sequence to reinforce COME. SIT is restrictive, and the dog is anxiously waiting to be released by COME, but SIT is different enough from WHOA to stand separately in the dog's mind.

Obedience trainers teach SIT by jerking up with the leash while jabbing down on the hips, but this could be confusing to our dog.

Obedience trainers use a choke chain and leash to teach SIT. They jerk up on the leash while jabbing down on the hips with the thumb and first finger of the left hand. We have used the upward pull or jerk to Speed Train WHOA. Using it now to teach SIT would confuse the dog.

Buckshot won't associate any of the SIT moves with WHOA if we trip the hind legs with a foot and push against the chest. Practice on the ground cable for better control.

Place your left foot and shin behind the dog's rear legs, command SIT, and push against his chest with your right hand. If he tries to back up when you push, your foot and shin will trip his hind legs, so he'll automatically sit. If he doesn't try to back up, he's still tripped into sitting when you push. After a little practice, the dog understands SIT.

Some dogs learn to stay seated better if the STAY command is added. The traffic cop gesture and slight upward pull on the cord (with the dog already seated) will not be confused with WHOA, but will add the understanding that he is not to move.

You may prefer that the dog remains seated with only the SIT command. Some dogs learn to stay more quickly, however, if the STAY command is added. As with WHOA, walk in front and around the dog, gradually increasing the distance until the dog is reliably obeying.

Walk partway down the ground cable, then command COME and enforce it with the check cord. Make a downward motion with your arm to add body gesture to the command. Use the staccato whistle interchangeably with the voice command.

The ground cable can help you with this. Do the SIT on one end of the cable. Command STAY, and walk beyond that end of the cable. He can't follow. When the dog on SIT will allow you to circle him, you can walk part way down the cable and command COME. He'll probably be anxious to do so. If you're having trouble with STAY, thump the front of the dog's chest with the flat of your hand for emphasis as you give the command.

If you must teach SIT-STAY before the dog is perfect on WHOA-HEEL, then do the SIT-COME sequence on a different day and in a different location.

Whether it's SIT-STAY or WHOA, a thump on the chest is a good reinforcement for a restrictive command.

By this time your dog has had extensive WHOA training and should be responding perfectly to the command. If not, don't start SIT-COME training because you don't want him to confuse the two commands. If you still need to practice WHOA-HEEL, it's best to postpone SIT-COME. If you insist on teaching SIT-COME before the dog is perfect on WHOA-HEEL, then do the two sequences at different locations and on different days.

Tip: If your dog is not responding to a particular command, make him earn everything he wants by obeying that command. One of my dogs hated to sit and tried every way he could to avoid it while training. It reached the point where I'd have to exert more pressure than our relationship could stand if I used discipline to enforce SIT. So if he wanted to be petted, I said SIT. If he did, he was petted and praised. Every evening, I said SIT as I came toward him with the food bowl. If he sat, I kept coming. If he didn't, I stopped. The change in that dog's attitude toward SIT was amazing, and it was accomplished without stress to either of us.

This tactic works when teaching any command. One of my dogs was having difficulty with COME – as many year-old dogs do – so I had him drag a check cord with a looped end to catch on things. When we hunted in fairly heavy cover, he was always hung up. I'd prepare by untangling enough cord so I could release him quickly. Then I'd call COME. He didn't want to the first time, so I pulled him in. GOOD BOY, I said when he got there, and followed it with ALL RIGHT as I released him. After a few days of obeying the command to get himself untangled, his attitude toward COME changed. This dog, that once ignored food if he had to get it by obeying COME, was now obeying the command under any circumstance.

Canine signal flag: A boxer watches his opponent's eyes instead of his gloves because eyes often telegraph intentions. A dog's intentions are often signaled by his tail, and knowing what's on his mind can help you nip disobedience in the bud. If the last half of a dog's tail dips downward upon hearing COME, he does not intend to obey.

Step 22

Down

At one time DOWN was essential. Dogs were taught to drop instead of stand when pointing birds, and for a very practical reason. Downed dogs were out of the way of nets the hunters would cast over a covey. Today, DOWN has no place in the hunt, but it can be handy while the dog is in the house or your vehicle.

Start DOWN from SIT and gently pull Buckshot's front legs out from under him.

At first, you may have to press down on the dog's hips to make him understand that DOWN means to stay there until further notice.

Start DOWN training with SIT. He's half-way down already. Say DOWN, then very gently, so you don't startle him into a struggle, pull both front legs out from under him. Pour on the petting and praise, even though you may have to restrain him by the collar at first.

You can speed his response by using bits of baked liver until he gets the idea. Pull his legs out with one hand, and bring the liver down below his nose with the other. He'll drop more willingly if his nose is following a goody. Give it to him when all the way down. When he learns the command, phase out the rewards, substituting them with praise.

Step 23

Force Fetch

Those hunters whose pups retrieved naturally during the first season, and who don't really care if their dogs are steady to shot, are excused from this session of class. I wish I could join you, too, instead of fooling with force fetch. I know it's the right thing to do for some dogs, but I hate it. As our kids grew older, it became clear that we raised five "only" children—and my dogs seem to have the same idea. Although they don't always care to do what I'm suggesting, they make it clear that they have great love for me and that each one firmly believes I love them the best of all. Altogether too often, when I have to pinch an ear to force train, instead of opening the mouth to wince, howl, or try to bite, my dog will just keep his mouth shut, take the pain, and look up lovingly at me as if saying, "If you want to pinch my ear, it's OK. I don't mind."

OK. I know. Force fetch is essential if the dog doesn't retrieve naturally, if you want him to be—and stay—steady to shot, if he tries to run off with birds or eat them, if he retrieves but is hardmouthed, or even if he's just a dominant, willful dog contesting you for pack leadership. It's a fact that once accomplished, force training makes ol' Buckshot "your" dog. What it initially, albeit temporarily, does to a great relationship, however, is where I have trouble. Once it's all over, the dog is more devoted to you than ever before. Fear of pain no longer has anything to do with it; he simply holds you in higher esteem.

Sometimes jealousy can motivate a bird dog to retrieve. Buckshot watches from confinement as a Lab pup fetches.

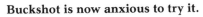

Buckshot is now anxious to try it.

Hey! It's fun!

Nevertheless, I confess that I'll try every trick in the book to avoid inflicting pain for no good reason that my dog can understand. My first attempt at avoiding the issue will be a monkey-see, monkey-do affair. I'll do some play fetch with a Labrador retriever while my bird dog watches the fun from confinement. There's always the chance that what didn't seem exciting before will look like great sport when another dog is getting to do it and he isn't. If I get him started, fine. I'll lead it into retrieving birds. It's possible that force training will never be necessary, but I can always do it later if problems arise.

If the envy ploy doesn't work, there are indirect methods. Some dogs do not seem to associate you with pain or discomfort when your hand isn't making direct physical contact. How many dogs understand that you are nevertheless responsible is anybody's guess. Anyhow, a number of dogs do not hold you to blame for indirect discomfort as much as they do pain resulting from a hands-on ear pinch.

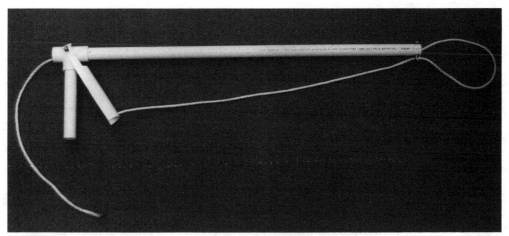

I made a Fetch-N-Forcer out of 24 inches of one-half-inch PVC pipe, a **T**, 6 inches of PVC for a handle, a cotterkey, and a half of a plastic drain fitting for the grip.

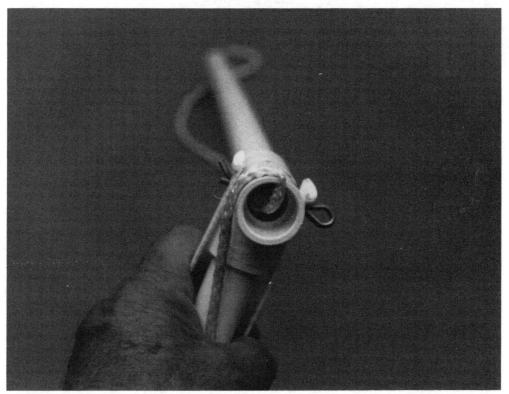

To use, pull the cord snug on the dog's neck, slide it into a narrow notch in the **T**, and hold the cord against the handle and under the palm.

The Fetch-N-Forcer works for me on some dogs but not others.

Assuming that neck constriction would gag the dog and make him open his mouth for air, I bought some plumbing parts and assembled a "Fetch-N-Forcer"—the design is loosely based on a farmer's hog catcher. Nylon cord has too much stretch, so it doesn't work; I used polyester. Slide the loop over the dog's head, snug it up, wrap the excess cord around the handle under your grip, say FETCH, and squeeze the handle.

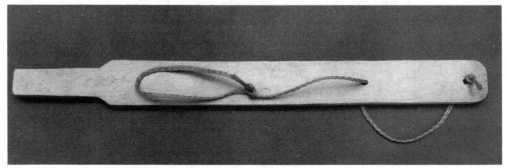

Webster Price invented his "training yoke" back in the 1920s.

Like my Fetch-N-Forcer, the yoke only works for me on some dogs.

Later, I was reading an old book and discovered that I had sort of reinvented the wheel. Trainer Webster Price had used a similar method in the 1920s. He cut a 3-inch wide paddle about 33 inches long out of three-quarter-inch lumber, placing two holes about 7 inches apart in the wide end. About 30 inches of cord passes through the holes and back to the handle on the back side of the paddle where a loop is formed.

It is claimed that Price had good luck opening dogs' mouths just by jerking on the loop with two fingers of the hand that held the paddles. That may work with strange dogs, but it doesn't work on dogs which I have handled a lot. Because the paddle is 3 inches wide, however, twisting it adds considerable constriction on the cord, and that may work better with some dogs and trainers. With either the Price method or my Fetch-N-Forcer, some of my dogs have stood there taking it until their eyes nearly bugged before responding. When it seems that I'll have to administer more pain than I would with the ear pinch to get results, I switch to something else with that dog.

One possibility is Delmar Smith's nerve hitch. Delmar benches the dog, has the collar snapped to a wire, then ties a cord to a front leg. After a half-hitch is also tied around the center two toes of the foot, the cord is pulled downward. The toes are pinched together to provide the pain or discomfort, but something else happens here. The dog seems to panic a bit, feeling out-of-control as they do when a foot is in a steel trap. The mouth comes open to protest.

Delmar invited me to one of his marvelous training seminars back in the early '70s, and I watched the system work on one dog after another. For me, it only works on strange dogs. Most of my own dogs stand there and take that, too.

Let's begin the force fetch process. Most trainers bench their dogs so that the dogs feel less secure and are more willing to cooperate. Inside a building is better than outside because there are fewer distractions. A short chain fastened to the wall can restrain the dog during the early lessons. If you must train outside, you can begin on the steel drum with the check cord over the limb for restraint.

The first step is showing the dog that you want him to open his mouth and take the buck. While dummies can be used to force train retrievers, bird dogs weren't selected for fetching in field trials for many years (and still aren't in the major horseback trials) so they have much poorer retrieving instincts and more problems such as hardmouth. The hard buck discourages chewing.

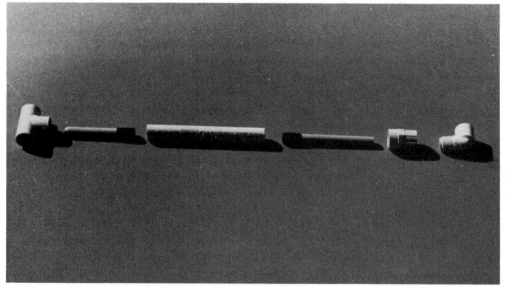

I made a buck out of 6½ inches of one-half-inch PVC, a T, a threaded elbow and fitting, and two one-half-inch wooden dowels 4 and 5 inches long.

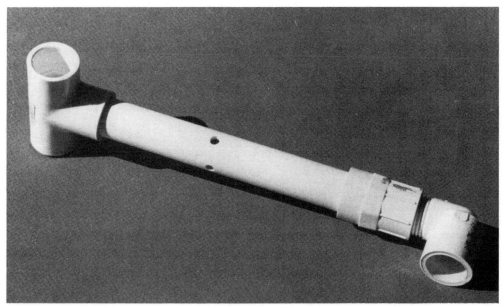

When assembled the buck looks like this. One end will always be above ground enough for a dog to pick it up easily when training has progressed that far.

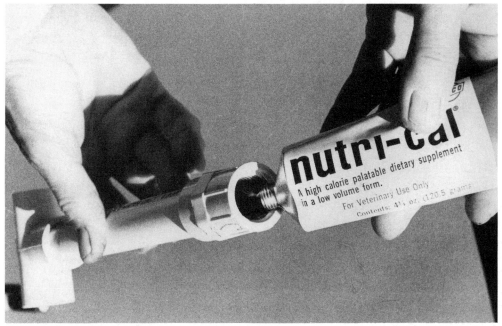

One end can be unscrewed and the dowel removed to insert Nutri-Cal or ground liver and grease.

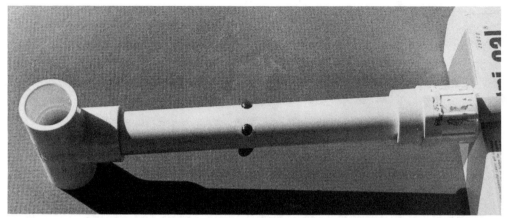

Reinsert the dowel plunger and screw the elbow back in place lightly. Now the goody can be squeezed from the holes by tightening the elbow another partial turn.

The buck can be a hunk of hardwood hoe handle. I assemble mine of plumbing parts which has an added advantage: I can load it with a goody to help the lesson along. Holes can be drilled into the center where the buck is gripped by the dog. The pipe can be partially filled with the palatable Nutri-cal, used cooking grease, or even boiled liver ground in the blender and mixed with grease—whatever your dog finds most tasty. Turn the threaded end against the dowel plunger to squirt some of the goody up through the holes. Let the dog smell the buck and even give it a tentative lick before proceeding.

Pressing the lips against the teeth will open Buckshot's mouth.

End the discomfort to the lips the instant the buck enters the dog's mouth.

A finger under the **V** of Buckshot's jaw will stop him from expelling the buck.

Grip the dog's muzzle with your left hand, and press the upper lips against his teeth with your thumb and fingers as you say FETCH and bring the buck just under his nose. Buckshot will open his mouth to stop the discomfort you're causing to his lips. Stick the buck in his mouth. Before the buck can be expelled by the dog's tongue, stick your right index finger into the V of the lower jawbone, and maintain an upward pressure. When he tries to expel the buck, push upward harder so he won't succeed. Count to yourself for about 15 seconds, then say GIVE, release your pressure on his chin, and accept the buck. A few confused dogs won't release it. Just twist the buck in his mouth, or raise one end. He'll let go. Don't get rough. Praise him for a good job.

Repeat this several times, but don't keep it up for more than 10 or 15 minutes. You can have one session a day, or two or three, but each lesson should be short.

When Buckshot has had a few days of this, he probably understands FETCH, but won't show it by opening his mouth on his own. He *will* show that he understands GIVE, by releasing the buck on command. At this point, begin teaching HOLD IT. Remove your finger from his chin as you would when saying GIVE but this time say HOLD IT! He won't, but don't let him drop it. The instant he tries, chuck or tap him under the chin with another HOLD IT. If he's quicker than you, pop that buck (or another that's perhaps handier) back into his mouth with the HOLD IT command.

Keep this up until Buckshot holds it until told GIVE. Make the hold longer and longer each time. When it's up to a minute or two, practice FETCH, HOLD IT, and GIVE next to the bench or drum. When he's holding, try to walk him at heel carrying the buck. If he tries to expel it, HOLD IT should change his mind at this point. If not, return the buck to his mouth immediately, and give him a good rap under the chin with your accompanying HOLD IT.

When Buckshot will walk at heel with the buck in his mouth, he's ready for the next step. He knows that you want him to open his mouth when you say FETCH. He also knows that you'll put the buck between his jaws as soon as his mouth is open; he doesn't care for that, so his hearing fails. You can go right to the ear pinch to improve his hearing, or you can use an intermediate trick. The idea of the trick is to startle the dog into opening his mouth rather than cause him pain. It's easier on your relationship.

I first thought of this one day when I had an air gun attached to a compressor. I benched a dog, put my left arm over his neck so he couldn't scoot backward to get away, then held the air gun between the lips at the left side of his jaw. As I brought the buck to his nose and said FETCH, I shot a blast of air between his teeth that fairly exploded his mouth open.

A vibrator with a blunted nail through the attachment will startle a dog's mouth open.

Not everybody has a compressor, so I searched for something else. *Do not use canned air.* This has fluorocarbons in it, and you don't want a sick or dead dog. Finally, I thought of a vibrator such as you might have to massage sore muscles. Mine had one hard plastic attachment which I've never used. I drilled a hole in its end the diameter of a fairly large nail. Then I cut off the point of a nail and rounded the edges with a file. (You don't want to cut or puncture skin in the dog's mouth.) Next, I shoved the nail through the plastic attachment. The head of the nail stopped it from going all the way through, of course. When I screwed the attachment onto the vibrator and switched it on, the nail buzzed like a snake tail.

I'm sure you're way ahead of me. I slipped the nail between the dog's teeth and over the tongue. Again, my left arm prevented him from scooting backward. As I expected, when I said FETCH, the mouth clamped shut. But, boy, did it open when I flicked on the vibrator. There was still no pain involved, but the vibrator was about three times as effective as the compressed air.

Timing is essential. The vibrator must stop or be removed the instant the buck enters the dog's mouth.

Whether you go right to the ear pinch or startle his mouth open, be sure to get your timing right. The idea here is that the pain or discomfort ends the *instant* the buck goes into the dog's mouth. Eventually, he learns to outsmart the pain and prevent it by grabbing the buck before discomfort begins. FETCH is his clue. If he reacts fast enough after hearing FETCH, he can avoid the pinch or the startling vibration. The sequence is FETCH followed by pain, then release of pain when the mouth opens and the buck goes in. There's no further need to sweeten the buck with Nutri-cal or grease when the ear pinch begins.

The ear has to be pinched in the right place to be effective on most bird dogs. The goody in the buck will make taking it more acceptable, but your dog won't reach for it. He'll only lick if it's offered, so you'll have to pinch his ear to get the mouth open, then release the pinch the instant the buck enters. Soon he'll be reaching for the buck to avoid the pinch.

The ear pinch has to be done right, or it won't work on a great many bird dogs. If the lower flap is pinched, Buckshot is likely to just stand there looking at you. Lay the ear back. You'll see a ridge. Hold the collar against the back side of the ear with your fingers, and press your thumbnail against the ridge. When that ridge is pinched between the collar and thumbnail, the mouth should open. If your dog resists, try the buckle and thumbnail. Dan Shimer, a Highland, Illinois, trainer who enjoys Shoot-to-Retrieve trials, says he doesn't have enough thumbnail to make the pinch. He fastens a bolt through the collar, then presses the ear against the bolt with his thumb. Arizona trainer, Bill West, uses a beer-can tab on his thumb instead of his thumbnail. The thin edge of the metal tab develops a sensitive spot on the ear that speeds the dog's reaction time.

When Buckshot is grabbing the buck to beat a pinch, hold it an inch or so away so he has to reach for it. Gradually make him reach increasingly farther, and then increasingly lower until the buck has to be picked up from the bench. You'll obviously have to loosen his restraint as this progresses.

The dog will have difficulty picking up a simple buck that lies flat on the table. That problem is easily solved, however, with the buck made of plastic plumbing parts. There's a T on one end and an L on the other. If the L is positioned at right angles to T, one end stands up off the ground. It was never necessary to glue these parts together, so a better assembly is to replace the L with another T. You don't need the plunger and L to help deliver goodies through the holes, and two Ts at right angles will raise one end higher.

When Buckshot will run down the bench to fetch the buck, he's ready for retrieving on the ground.

After the dog is reaching down to the bench to grab the buck, start moving it farther and farther down the bench. Soon Buckshot will run to the end of the bench to fetch the buck. At that point, he's ready for retrieving on the ground at progressively longer distances.

You must be consistent or force training will drag out forever. To get results, you need to resolve to spend up to 15 minutes *every day* for however long it takes. Most intelligently submissive dogs have it down pat in three weeks, but willful, dominant types, and slow learners have taken two months and longer to learn the lesson.

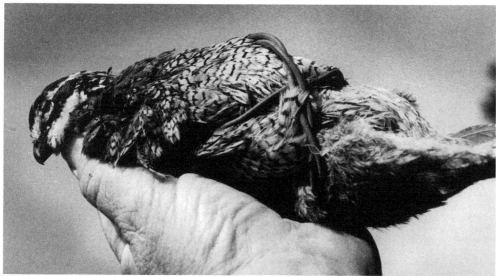

If your natural retriever is becoming a bit hardmouthed, but you don't want to force train, try Dan Thomason's idea of barbed wire wrapped around a game bird during fetch practice. The bird is easily carried without pain or discomfort provided the dog doesn't chomp down.

When you switch to birds in the field, Buckshot probably won't contest you for them. He has been well-drilled in FETCH and GIVE. If he does hang on, don't play tug of war; that promotes hardmouth. Blow in his ear or nose, or simply push the bird farther back into his mouth. Any of these methods will get you an immediate release.

Those owner/trainers who tried the indirect methods and found they worked may have temporary difficulty in the field. When a dog refuses a FETCH command, you need to make a correction, and the Webster Price yoke or Fetch-N-Forcer certainly isn't in your coat. You may have the cord to do the nerve hitch, but you won't have the time. You need to apply that correction within seconds, not minutes; otherwise the dog fails to grasp why he's being disciplined.

This does not mean that the indirect methods are worthless. Not every dog so trained will refuse you in the field. But if they do, so what! They understand that discomfort ends when the buck or bird goes into the mouth. It's time for a refresher when he gets home, but now do it with the ear pinch. This is more than discomfort. It's pain, so he quickly makes the bridge between the two methods. You've avoided the long, difficult part of the pain method, yet you now have a dog that can be corrected with an ear pinch in the field.

Step 24

Stop-to-Flush

We tend to teach dogs as little as we can get by with. We're busy people, and we think we can manage without the niceties. As a result, stop-to-flush is rarely taught, except to springer spaniels, and then only by professional trainers. Stop-to-flush, however, is more than a nicety. It's your insurance policy against accidental loss of the only thing that prevents Buckshot from being the world's widest ranging flushing dog: his pointing instinct.

How can teaching a flushing-dog nicety to a bird dog prevent him from acting like a spaniel? By allowing you to shoot over an accidental flush. Almost no hunter will ask whether the bird was bumped or properly pointed. The whir of wings triggers an almost automatic shooting response, and that bird is snatched out of the sky long before anyone wonders about the dog's manners and mistakes. Shoot just a few birds that a dog accidentally bumps, though, and very soon he will always bump birds. If he's taught stop-to-flush, you know when it's an honest mistake. He stops. If he's deliberately flushing, he'll chase. It's OK to shoot when he stops to flush because you're not encouraging flushing, and his pointing instincts remain intact.

Stop-to-flush is of least importance to Mearns and bobwhite-quail hunters. It is very important to grouse and other Western quail dogs, and it is extremely important to any pointing dog used to hunt pheasants.

A good place to begin this training is on the steel drum. Have some pigeons in a bag, box, or training vest. Make sure the wind is into the dog's face, and have the birds somewhere behind the dog so he's unaware of their presence. Place him on the drum, and snap the check cord from above onto his collar. He is long accustomed to standing on the drum, so it won't be necessary to command WHOA just yet.

Walk around him a bit as you did during WHOA training, then step back to the birds. Get one in a hand without him noticing. Return to the dog, and with an underhand motion, sling the pigeon a couple feet past Buckshot's nose and across his line of vision. Just as you let go, and the wings flap, command WHOA! It is split-second timing, but the sound of wings should be heard *before* the WHOA. They should be so close together, however, that the WHOA should hit Buckshot's ears just as his eyes start to bug. He'll probably hold because of

Stop-to-flush can begin back on the steel drum by teaching Buckshot that birds, too, mean WHOA. Next, switch to tossing birds with your dog beside the drum, then have him stop for thrown birds while Buckshot is on (and later off) the ground cable.

long familiarity with the drum, but if he doesn't, he'll be caught by the check cord and scrambling for footing. Place him back on the drum for the next bird. Three or four birds a session is enough.

In my experience, most dogs stand steady on the drum by the third bird. Do several sessions over the next few days anyway, to reinforce the lesson. After that, change to one bird while the dog is on the drum, and then the other two or three with him standing beside it.

When Buckshot is standing steady beside the drum for the thrown flushes, move to the ground cable. Snap both runner cable and check cord to the dog's collar so you have good control. You'll be walking with the dog, so have a helper (always downwind from the dog) throw the pigeon. You order WHOA, of course. Practice on the cable until the dog anticipates your WHOA command, and starts to halt the instant he hears or sees wings.

Once he understands that the flush is just one more way of commanding WHOA, and he is obedient to it, work him off cable, but still on the check cord. After a few times with the helper, switch to pigeons in bird launchers without the helper. Always lead the dog upwind of the launcher so he can't smell the bird. Without the helper around, he won't anticipate where the flush will come from. The surprise factor adds additional temptation to chase. When he stops to these flushes, cease giving the WHOA command. If he still consistently stops, you're on your way. Practice it another two weeks to make sure the habit is permanently entrenched.

Step 25

Handling Running Birds

Not every bird dog can learn to do a good job of trailing. Pointers and setters have been bred to hunt coveys. Such a dog runs with his head held high and seldom puts his nose to ground to track foot scent. This dog sometimes has trouble with single quail and birds that run. The versatile breeds have more hound blood and usually make good trailers. Of course, that can have its price, too. Some of those dogs become so preoccupied with trailing foot scent that they aren't aware of the covey until it's exploding all around them.

How your dog should handle running birds depends upon what is natural for him. Maybe you noticed his natural bent during the puppy-nose awakening. How did he act when you put your finger to the ground and he caught the scent he was supposed to find? Did he consistently trail it right to the goody? If he did, you have a trailer. If, instead, he cast about, testing the air with a high head until he located the treat, he's not a natural trailer. Some little pups trail for a time until leg growth raises their noses too high to smell ground scent. Rather than drop their noses to the ground unnaturally, they cast about for air scent after that.

To test a dog for natural ability to trail, or to determine if he might do better at circling birds, lay a scent trail. This dog scarcely dropped his head to catch the odor of chicken skin before he was on his way.

If you're uncertain about your dog, test him now. Drag a meat scrap about 15 feet, then drop it. Bring the dog close to the beginning of the trail, and calm him. Sit down with him, if necessary. Talk quietly and pet him until any excitement passes. Then place your finger on the start of the trail. If he doesn't respond, kneel and put your own nose near the trail's beginning. Scratch at that spot in the grass with your fingers. When he investigates, let him proceed without comment, which could excite him. If you've taught him FIND IT (if you haven't, you should) you can just show him the trail after he's calmed, and in a very matter-of-fact voice, give the command. Either way, you'll see his natural behavior in action if you haven't excited him.

Dogs that trail can be readily taught to follow running quail or pheasants. These dogs are usually slower and more methodical than the high-headed dogs. They seldom have the snap and dash to slam into a running-type bird and hold it, so it's better to teach them controlled trailing and stop-to-flush.

Dogs that locate by air scent are better at circling the birds than trailing. One circling method requiring a backing dog was discussed in Part 2 Step 18.

If you're teaching your dog to trail cripples, use ducks, on water and off. You'll have less trouble with Buckshot bumping birds he's expected to point.

Before teaching your dog to trail, ask yourself why you're doing it. If it's simply to trail cripples, then it's wise to train with a duck because he's not expected to point that species. He'll still become proficient at trailing, and he'll fetch your wing-tipped runners later on, but he's less likely to begin trailing and bumping the healthy birds he's supposed to point. Some dogs have been turned into bumpers by using dead game birds as drags. If you're training for cripples only, send him on the shackled duck's trail with the FETCH command. (If you decide to keep a duck, or ducks, for this purpose, keep in mind that ducklings must be fed *non-medicated* chicken-grower mash because medicated will kill them. Grown ducks can eat layer mash, but mine seem to prefer corn plus grass, other vegetation, and table scraps. They go wild over dead insects from my bug light.)

More likely, you're training the dog to trail because you're sick of pheasants or Western quail running out from under the point. Yes, you do risk creating a bumper, but that's why you will also train your dog to stop to both whistle and flush. Stop-to-whistle allows you to catch up when the dog is getting beyond gun range. Stop-to-flush permits you to shoot an accidental flush without ruining the dog's pointing ability. Teach these two things before trailing lessons begin.

The "versatile" breeds ordinarily do not have such strong pointing instincts that they will not drop their heads and follow ground scent.

Trailing

Once more, keep in mind that unlike tracking cripples, trailing healthy running birds is *not* fetch practice. He must learn to gingerly handle these birds, following when they run, stopping to point when they stop, and doing his best not to push the birds into flight. You can stop him with the single sharp blast on the whistle that he has learned means WHOA. You also must stop him when he's getting too far away, or when you know he's pressing birds too hard. If at some point your dog does catch a bird and delivers it, you certainly can't yell at him for retrieving. Accept the bird, but don't praise him. Hereafter make sure that you're following close enough and that you do your part in controlling him with the whistle.

My Nebraska friend, Roy Speece, starts teaching his dogs to handle running birds by working with robins on the lawn. The dog sight-points the robin, and moves up when the robin hops away. If the dog presses the robin, it flies, and Roy shows his disapproval vocally. If the robin simply flies through no fault of the dog, there is no vocal correction.

Harnessed pigeons can provide enough of a scent trail to start dogs on trailing, especially early in the day when dew is on the ground.

I've used harnessed pigeons for this purpose. Some pigeons don't run well, but the better ones can do a decent job. Start the bird in the open. Let the dog sight-point, and be prepared to WHOA him with the whistle if he presses too close. Keep the dog 15 or 20 feet back from the pigeon when possible. Later on, a pheasant in marshy cover may let a dog get within five or six feet, but a wild pheasant in dry land habitat will not often permit a dog's nose up his tail feathers.

When the pigeon moves away, release the dog from WHOA with ALL RIGHT. Make the dog stop every time the pigeon does.

I once found, and caught, a wing-crippled starling I used to train an English pointer. I freed the starling in an open field with almost no cover. If the pointer tried to move up too fast between points, I'd growl *"e-z-e-e-e"* to improve her caution. The starling was a great runner and my dog learned quickly.

Starlings are pest birds and as far as I know are legally live-trapped in any state. Check to be sure. If you try it, you'll have to shackle the wings, of course. Use a brightly colored yarn (orange is probably best) and let about a yard of it trail behind the wings so you or a helper can catch the starling to use again.

Whatever you use, don't continue this for too long. Once the dog learns to point and move up, always at a respectable distance, it's time to switch. Too much sight pointing is not a good thing. In fact, that's why we did all the training on scent pointing first and left trailing to well after the dog could be easily tempted into bad habits by a few pigeons or "stink" birds.

Shackled pheasants are great birds for training dogs to trail. This is not fetch practice, so keep Buckshot on a check cord until you're sure you have him under control.

For high-school-level scent trailing, a pheasant is the teacher. They're big, have a strong odor, and are Olympic-class runners. Keep one in a cage, and feed him a game-bird mix or pellets. If neither are available, laying mash for chickens will work just fine.

To train, first shackle the bird so it can't fly. Use about 20 feet of lightweight yellow (or other bright, easily seen color) ski cord, or check cord. Tie one end around the bases of both wings with a square knot to prevent flight. The long end will drag behind. Tie a loop in that end so it will tangle in cover and reduce the length of the first few trails.

Start the trail in the open, but within sight of fairly dense cover. The wind should be from the cover to you on the dog's first try. We want him to be successful, and the scent blowing toward him will make it much easier. Hold the pheasant to the ground. Pull three or four breast feathers, and drop them right there. Point the bird toward the heavy cover and let go.

If your dog is off check cord and ignores your efforts at control, you can't become angry when the dog proudly presents you with a dead pheasant, but you must go back to practicing controls.

As soon as the bird runs out of sight, bring your dog in on leash. Point to the feathers. When he sniffs them, say FIND IT in a very calm voice. When he starts the track, go with him. Hold onto the leash until you recognize that he has the scent trail and is calm enough to stay with it. If he's excitedly running helter-skelter, take him back to the start, quiet him for a few moments, and try it again. When he's concentrating, turn loose the leash.

The pheasant is fast on his feet, so you'll get some exercise, too. Keep up as best you can, and stop the dog with the whistle if he gets beyond shotgun range. ALL RIGHT him when you catch up. Your dog may get a point here and there, and then move on by himself, if the pheasant keeps running. If you catch up and find he's still pointing old scent of the pheasant that left, again move him on with ALL RIGHT.

Eventually, the pheasant will get his cord tangled. At this time, the dog should point, of course. If you have a helper, let him catch the pheasant and untangle the cord while you control the dog. You'll have to tie the dog if you're working alone. Bring the pheasant back to him for a sniff. Show by your petting and praise that you caught the bird through his efforts. Put the pheasant in your bag, and that's it for the day.

The next time, and thereafter, arrange the locations so the wind will be perpendicular to the scent trail. It won't be as easy for the dog, so he'll have to concentrate harder on trailing. You will, of course, start the bird in the open and head him toward cover as before. Your dog will either follow foot scent right where the bird ran or body scent several feet downwind of the actual trail. The choice is your dog's.

After your dog becomes good at this, and you become acquainted with your bird's stamina (and yours) you may want to remove the loop at the end of his cord so the pheasant runs farther before tangling.

All the while your dog is learning to trail, it would be wise to practice his stop-to-flush training with pigeons. By necessity the pheasant must be shackled or he wouldn't put down a trail. We can't flush him accidentally, or on purpose, so it's important to use other means to be certain that Buckshot won't later forget to stop to the flush of a wild bird.

Circling

Over the years, some intelligent dogs have learned to handle running birds by circling to the front. The birds suddenly see the dog and reverse direction. If the dog is very careful and quite smart, he'll gingerly herd the birds toward his hunter. When they find themselves seemingly trapped between hunter and dog, many of these running birds hold to point until flushed. Some birds, especially late in the season after being well-educated by other hunters, flush wildly. They've been already herded close enough for shooting, though.

Only very intelligent dogs learn to circle on their own; and they're often fairly old when it happens. So it makes sense that if a person is hunting a high-headed, non-trailing bird dog on Western quail or pheasants, he might want to try training his dog to circle.

First let me say that this is not commonly done. At one time it was thought that dogs couldn't be taught to circle. Chances are, not all can, but it's worth a try.

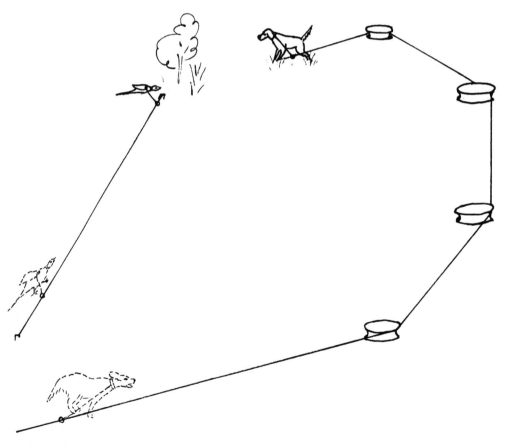

Teaching dogs to circle birds is not commonly attempted, but with plenty of practice this layout of ground cables can get Buckshot started.

You'll need two ground cables as indicated in the drawing: one – for the pheasant – is straight; the other – for the dog – swings out and loops back. The pheasant is shackled with about three feet of trailing cord that has a loop in the end. The bird is dizzied by shaking it back and forth with both your hands. When its head is wobbling, try placing it in light cover near the start of the cable. If it's dizzy enough to stay put, snap the runner cable to the cord loop. Wind direction must blow from the pheasant's cable to the dog's cable.

Bring the dog in on check cord to point the pheasant. When he does, attach the runner cable to his collar. Praise and handle him on point while waiting for the pheasant to wake up and sneak off. If your bird takes too long to awaken, place it in a low-cut cardboard box with a string attached. Jerk the string to move and awaken the pheasant.

When the pheasant runs, the dog may, too. If not, say ALL RIGHT and run along the dog's cable yourself. He'll follow your example. Let him run ahead to follow the circling cable to meet the bird while you cut across to the pheasant's cable. The bird will get to the end, find itself trapped between you and the dog and will usually hold for point.

Catch the bird, let the dog sniff, then return it to the cage.

If you try this, don't expect immediate results. It may take your dog two or three months to learn it. You'll have to train when the wind is right or keep moving the arrangement to suit the wind. It's best to arrange the dog's cable sometimes on one side of the pheasant's cable and sometimes on the other when the wind has changed. The dog should learn to always circle on the downwind side of the bird to help keep track of the bird's movement by scent. Not all dogs will do this, however. Many dogs show a natural or automatic preference for circling to left or right, (just as some of you may automatically go to the left or right side of a church or theater).

Scott's aircraft-type ground cable will require several auto-wheel rims staked in place to form the circling shape of the dog's cable. The pheasant requires a separate cable that is straight and shorter than the dog's. Shackle the bird's wings and fasten the rope shackle to the slider cable. Pheasants are not as large and strong as dogs, of course, so they're more easily stopped when the slider cable catches on a weed or clump of grass. Make sure that the vegetation under and beside the pheasant's cable is trimmed short and that the area is free of obstructions.

Step 26

Hunt Conditioning

Most bird dogs can handle a day's hunt without pre-conditioning. They'll probably slow down somewhat on day two of a full weekend. If you take a week-long hunt during bird season, however, it's either get your dog in shape, or do without him for half the week.

A variety of methods are used to condition dogs. Jogging or walking with your dog is fine for you, but does little to exercise him. Some owners have their dogs drag chains or sacks of rocks. Other dogs stay in shape pulling sleds or carts. I like "roading" because I think it best exercises those muscles that are normally used while running during the hunt.

Roading the dog beside the car will condition his lungs and muscles for all-day hunting if you gradually build up to three miles a day.

Choose a dirt road, if you can. You probably can't because there aren't many left, but at least pick a road with almost no traffic. Regardless of the type of road, start with one-half-mile a day and gradually increase the distance. Be extra careful on blacktop or concrete; they're hard on pads. Check your dog's feet each day to make sure they're getting tougher and not wearing through. If they do become sore, stop this exercise until they heal.

Before you start, recognize that Buckshot will not raise two fingers and ask permission when he has to relieve himself. He'll squat without warning, and he won't think about the consequences to his head or your arm which are connected by an eight-foot-long leash or cord. Keep a constant eye on your dog, and be prepared to stop in an instant. Keep your other eye open, too, for other vehicles so you can pull onto the shoulder and hold Buckshot safely by the side of your car.

Choose a seldom-traveled road and drive at a rate that makes your dog lope to keep up.

Drive at a speed that makes your dog lope to keep up. It shouldn't be a lazy lope or a trot, but don't run him as hard as he can go. The correct speed is when he's feeling somewhat pressured to keep up.

A very effective Band-Aid for failure to condition is vitamin C. The best is ester C, which is made by Inter-Cal Corporation and probably will be sold under the name C Flex. (Address in appendix.) It contains metabolites that get the C into the bloodstream about an hour more quickly and keep it in the tissues longer than ordinary vitamin C.

Muscle soreness is caused by microscopic tears in the tissues. Rebuilding the tissues requires collagen, which requires vitamin C, which is therefore used in great quantity during extreme exercise. If you get this extra C into the bloodstream before the hunt (at least an hour, a day is better, and some say a week is best) then the rebuilding process begins as soon as the tears occur. Most of the soreness that might have stopped the dog (or you) never occurs. Excess C, if there is any, passes in the urine.

I found that 12 grams a day works best for my own body when I'm hunting all day in rugged territory such as mountains. I take three grams before going, another three at noon, three in midafternoon, and the final three in the evening. I weigh about 175 pounds, so I calculate a 50 or 60-pound dog probably needs one-third of that or four grams a day. I think giving a gram (two 500mg tablets or at least three 300mg tablets) four times a day is best. I also have been successful, however, breaking it into three doses: one before the hunt, another at noon, and the last one after the hunt. I gave three 500mg or five 300mg tablets per dose in those instances. Exact doses are not important with C, but keep track of how much you do give. If you give, or take, more than the body is using, it loosens the bowels. Should that occur, simply reduce the dose a bit.

After I had written about using C in this manner several times, readers began to surprise me with reports of its effectiveness on dogs with joint problems. Dogs that used to become lame after several hours were hunting day after day. I later found out that ester C was developed by a man who was searching for a cure to his wife's arthritis. Following that, I discovered California veterinarian Dr. Wendell Belfield, who successfully used vitamin C to prevent hip dysplasia in eight litters of German shepherd pups from parents that had HD themselves or that had thrown dysplastic pups before.

Vitamin C is no cure-all, but considering that it is just a component of food, it does some incredible things. I'm told that C has some 300 functions in the body. The dog can make some of its own C in its liver, but not nearly enough when the needs are extreme. The human body makes none.

It would be best to condition, *and* use C during extreme and prolonged exercise. I have seen out of shape dogs actually become conditioned, though, while taking C during a several-day-long hunt. Instead of wearing out, they improved each day. The same thing has happened to me. I have been out of condition from sitting while writing for weeks on end, yet after about three days of hunting, I'd be feeling so good I'd forget to take the C a fourth to a half of the time.

Step 27

Year Two

My guess is that more than one of you whose spring-born pup started beautifully at 8 to 16 weeks—and even hunted well that fall—got a disappointment somewhere between 8 and 14 months. It was time for serious training, time to build upon what he already knew, but he seemed like a changed dog. At first, it seemed as if he had forgotten everything he knew. Then perhaps you realized that his memory was just fine; it was more like he thought he was too big to have to do that "puppy stuff" anymore. He had better ideas now. About that time your own memory jogged. Of course! He had entered puberty and was acting like an 11 to 13-year-old child. So you reminded the dog that he lives here, he eats your food, and the rules haven't changed. In fact, the rules tightened, training became more serious, and you overcame his irresponsible attitude toward life.

He was a vastly better dog when his second hunting season rolled around. You breathed a sigh of relief. Puberty was history, the present seemed bright, and your projection for the future was "to live happily ever after."

Now he's 22 to 24 months old. Disaster has struck. Your day-to-day association with the dog seems to be deteriorating into a contest of wills. His blockheadedness of about a year ago was mild stuff by comparison. The dog, especially if he's a male, is trying to displace you as pack leader. Talk about forgetting his training! He's trying to train you! It's as if he's an 18 to 22-year-old boy preparing to leave home and lead his own pack.

Leave home is exactly what many dogs do at age two. Their owners can't believe what they're seeing. These once great dogs have gone hopelessly backward! Sinister ideas occur to otherwise fair men. There are people out there who remember a great hunt with this dog, they don't know about his backsliding. Maybe they'd buy him if the price were right.

So the dog is sold. More dogs change hands at age two than at any other time beyond puppyhood. And guess what! Somebody else has the dog a few months, and the blacksliding reverses itself. You don't have the last laugh because the other fellow has a fine hunting dog and you got taken for two years of food and veterinary care, plus all your hours of training.

My rule is simple: If the pup showed early promise and progressed as expected during training, I'm confident he'll return to as good or better than he was before this obnoxious stage in his development. Time will cure much of the problem but it's also important to inform Buckshot who's running the pack at this house. Go back to the canine behavioral moves in Part 2 Step 12 to recharge his memory.

Another excellent thing to do at this time, if you haven't done it already, is force-fetch training. Your relationship is already in a deteriorated state due to the dog's behavior. Force training will temporarily deteriorate it further, but after a while, you'll begin to notice a change. Odds are, at the end of force training, that rebellious dog will have become "your" dog, a more loyal, faithful follower than you thought possible.

As fall approaches, a spring-born two-year-old will be nearing his third season in the field. Do a brush-up on obedience, and work a few birds before opening day. He isn't mature yet, and won't be until about three years old. Without a tune-up, he might not perform as well as you would like or as well as he can. Some dogs need a pre-season reminder every year. Training retention varies widely between breeds and even more so between individual dogs. An annual brush-up can only improve your dog's performance.

Keeping Pigeons for Training

Pigeons can be kept in any reasonably tight shed or building corner where a pen can be built. My favorite makeshift pigeon loft, until rot finally destroyed it, was an old, retired truck camper that started coming apart at the seams from long, hard use. I could open the windows and ceiling vent to whatever degree was appropriate to the day's temperatures. The openings were screened, so the pigeons couldn't engage in unauthorized flight. A 2-by-4-foot plywood landing ramp was attached outside and below one window that had the screen removed. I simply opened that window when I wanted to fly the birds for exercise. When training, I caged the number I needed, then opened the window so they could fly back in after returning from field duty.

When I opened the entrance window after catching birds for training, all the rest of my pigeons also could exit from that window. I live in the country, so I didn't mind. In town, however, allowing free flight for too much of the day can cause you people problems. Pigeons often take a fancy to parading on neighbors' roofs and fertilizing them. This can be prevented by the use of "bobs" at the entrance window.

A bob is a metal rod suspended at one end. A group of bobs slide onto another rod, and the assembly covers the inside of the entrance window. Because the bottoms of the bobs are not fastened, they swing inward when returning birds push against them, allowing entry into the loft. A stop inside the window prevents the bobs from swinging outward, however, so it's a one-way door. Returning training pigeons may enter, but inside birds can't exit to sit on roofs.

Any shed or small building can house pigeons, but this one is engineered for quick recovery of the birds. Pickets prevent loafing on the roof. The birds must return to the landing board, after which they can be herded through the bobs and into the loft.

A set of bobs (available in Scott's catalog) can be placed over any opening in any kind of structure that houses pigeons. To keep your training birds from loafing on roofs instead of going right to their loft, train late in the day. As soon as you have finished training, shake a partially filled coffee can of feed to announce dinnertime, then walk inside to fill the feeder. If the birds are trained to the coffee can, they'll be through the bobs and inside almost as soon as you arrive.

Some trainers trap pigeons around grain elevators and make no effort to keep them or raise more. The birds are shot during training, and those that escape probably return to their old haunts. In that case, there's no need for bobs or much else besides a simple shed. If you plan to reuse some of the pigeons in training, and you can, then they must become accustomed to your loft so they will call it home. That takes two weeks of confinement in the building for common pigeons, or breeds such as rollers. After that, they'll always return to your loft. Should you buy homing pigeons, you'll never be able to release them because they'll return to their old homes, even years later. The young they raise, however, will always come back to your loft.

Start the coffee-can conditioning during this two-week confinement. Just shake the can before feeding. Give the birds as much grain as they clean up in 20 or 30 minutes during morning and evening mealtimes.

Grain mixes specifically for pigeons are available at feed stores and elevators. When mixes are unavailable, I've been very successful feeding birds whole corn, wheat, and milo. The amount of corn they consume varies with the season – as much as one-half of the total grain consumption in cold weather, and as little as one-fourth during hot weather. Do not feed them cracked corn (commonly called chicken scratch), because any that's scattered and not cleaned up has a tendency to mold and cause illness if eaten later.

It's easiest to let the birds decide how much they need of each grain. After the feeding period, remove any remaining food. If neighbors are not a problem, and mice don't get into the grain, you can feed once a day, rather than twice, in whatever amount the birds clean up. Or you can keep the various grains before them at all times in a cafeteria feeder with separate compartments for each grain. Pigeon food pellets are sometimes available, but they are more expensive than grains and the birds have to be taught to eat it by mixing with grains in the beginning.

I raise young birds to shoot during training sessions and use my breeders for training only when dead birds aren't required. They fly back to the loft and continue their business of propagation. Obviously you must not upset their nests or their eggs will not hatch. This is easily accomplished, however. You simply need to know that cocks sit on the eggs from 10 A.M. to 4 P.M. The hens, as seems to be the case throughout nature, get the bum end of the domestic deal and sit from 4 P.M. to 10 A.M. Never use the hens or cocks for training when it's their time to incubate eggs.

Chances are, some of the pigeons will be spooked from their eggs when you enter the loft to catch birds. It would be easy to grab the wrong ones, so you need to be able to differentiate between cocks and hens. You can do this in advance by observing who is on the nest at what time, keeping in mind that pigeons do not observe daylight savings. Cocks also identify themselves by their characteristic *kook-uh-la-coo* as they strut, bowing and turning in circles.

If you have many birds, you probably won't be able to remember each, so band them. Special leg bands are available from pigeon-supply catalogs. You can choose different colors to easily distinguish cocks from hens. I seldom have bands when I need them, so I go to the hardware or building-supply store and buy a foot of plastic tubing of appropriate width. (The inside must fit comfortably on the pigeon's leg.) I slice off one-quarter-inch lengths of tubing, then cut a split into each so they can be opened to snap on the birds' legs. With hens banded on their left legs and cocks on their right, I always know which bird to grab.

This loft has nest boxes with doors to keep young birds from using them as extra perches until they're ready to mate.

While this boxed arrangement is just providing resting areas for young birds, it would easily convert to simple nest boxes. Just fasten 3- or 4-inch boards across the front to keep the squabs from falling out.

Nest boxes should be about 12-by-12-by-24 inches, big enough to allow the hen to start a new nest before the previous pair of squabs are ready to leave. Pigeons are energetic breeders. The hen lays two eggs which take about 21 days to hatch.

Pigeons are hearty birds and have few illnesses if caution is exercised against bringing in disease with new birds. Feeders and waterers should have covers which prevent pigeons from perching on top and depositing droppings inside. Other than that, cleanliness is not a major factor in health. In fact, uninformed advice to the contrary, weekly clean-up is a good way to *cause* illness in your loft. Several inches of their own *dry* droppings has proven to be a safeguard against poor health. Dry is the key word. A moist floor is the worst possible environment for pigeons. Avoid a dirt floor because even a deep layer of droppings will become moist during the rainy season. In my experience, droppings on wood or concrete remain dry enough. Perhaps a sheet of plastic over dirt, then a layer of sand would also keep moisture out of the droppings.

Homers are the strongest flyers, and if trained, they'll come home from any distance. If your training ground is many miles away, just start dropping off young birds along the way—first at 1 mile, then 2, 5, 10, 15, and so on, until they learn the whole route.

Rollers are not as strong as homers, but they're small, easy keepers, and their aerobatics will fascinate you. They do quick backward somersaults while in flight! Some do single flips, but the better birds continue spinning long enough to fall perhaps 50 feet before resuming level flight. Be warned. If you keep pigeons for training, it's very likely you'll soon find yourself keeping these birds just because you like them.

The Pointing Labrador Retriever

I'm giving the pointing Labrador retriever full-chapter status because it seems to be a phenomenon whose time has come. A few pointing Labs have always popped up here and there, but they were regarded as novelties or as faulty retrievers. Nobody tried to breed them. There were plenty of pointing breeds more suitable to the conditions of the time.

Mayo Kellogg made no effort to breed pointing Labs, either, but the trait materialized in his strain many years ago. Pointing is a recessive gene, so dogs that didn't point themselves, but carried the genes, would produce some pups that point, if mated with another Lab that carried the gene. Gradually, pointing became fairly widespread among Kellogg's dogs. And the hunters who bought them were quite enthusiastic about the surprise trait.

Mayo mentioned this to me several years ago, and eventually, almost reluctantly, I wrote about pointing Labs in *Outdoor Life*. I knew that these eager-to-please, easy-to-train, short-range dogs would be perfect for many hunters, but I expected flack from Lab breeders who still believe pointing retrievers should be culled.

The response to that article was incredible! One young boy wrote a critical letter, probably reflecting his father's opinion. But within a month, or so, more than 2,000 other people communicated their enthusiasm to me and Mayo. A Canadian reader was delighted because he had always insisted that, if it could be found or developed, a pointing Lab would be the ideal gun dog for most hunters. Many letters and calls were from people who wanted such a dog, but many others were from folks who already owned them. Their enthusiasm quickly resulted in a pointing Lab rendezvous in South Dakota where dogs could be certified and where future plans for the pointing strain might be formulated.

Pointing Labrador retrievers may not have the style of bird dogs, but they're proving to be highly versatile and useful to the hunters who own them.

While I don't foresee many confirmed bird-doggers switching to pointing Labs, reader response has made it quite clear that this dog will fill a real need among other hunters. Many first-time owners are more comfortable with short-ranging dogs; in fact, they're often downright nervous about their ability to control even a moderately wide-running dog. Others, in today's shrinking habitat, require a very close dog to avoid trespass problems. The Lab is already very versatile – retrieving anything you shoot and willing to quarter the uplands as a surrogate spaniel. Add pointing to that and you have one very practical, if not spectacular, hunter. On pheasants, especially, these dogs excel.

The big question, obviously, is how should pointing Labs be trained? They are still primarily retrievers and water dogs at that. Many, we hope most, will continue to retrieve waterfowl as well as upland game. Is there a way that you can take advantage of the pointing instinct without subordinating any other good Lab qualities? I think there is.

Mayo Kellogg protests that my article suddenly thrust him into being considered the number one authority on pointing Labs while he doesn't know very much more than anyone else. That's not quite true. Mayo is a third-generation breeder with both accumulated family knowledge and an intuitive understanding of what will connect with the minds of individual dogs. This is evident even in his choice of dogs. You rarely see Mayo with a finished dog, or working at finishing a dog. He is always starting a youngster—always excited over what will grab this new pup's mind.

Mayo's opinion, based on both his own experience and the way his father trained Labradors as pheasant dogs, is that the pup should be worked hard on *sight* retrieves in the water—but not on land. These water retrieves teach the dog to be aware, to watch, and to mark the falls—and this ability will carry over onto land retrieves later. Mayo believes, however, that land retrieves should be handled by scent. Give a dog a couple of sight fetches so he understands that he will retrieve on land as well as water. After that, all land retrieves are "blinds." Either toss them into high grass or weeds when the pup isn't looking or plant the dummies ahead of time. He finds them by searching. Eventually, the pup learns that his jobs on land and water are quite different. He may sight-fetch in water, but he hunts on land.

Mayo Kellogg (left) developed the first strain of pointing Lab. He and Doug Converse are approaching a yellow Lab pointing a pen-raised chukar.

Use pheasant-scented dummies on land. Either dose them with bottled scent, or tie wings to the dummies. Do a couple of sight fetches with these dummies to establish the odor in the dog's mind. Toss or plant the first blind retrieve just a few feet inside the cover, and make sure that the wind is blowing from the dummy to the dog. We want him to succeed, not just run a few feet after the FETCH command, then stop and stand confused because he realizes he didn't see anything thrown. The odor will draw him. Throw or plant scented dummies deeper and deeper into cover until the dog may have to search as much as 15 yards before he finds them.

Finally, you'll be able to walk into the wind, and your dog will search out planted dummies without being told FETCH. Insist that he deliver them to you, of course. Make sure, too, he never ranges more than about 15 yards before finding the next one. This will help establish a very short searching range.

A good pheasant dog must quarter well, so practice that according to either the instructions in this book or in *Speed Train Your Own Retriever*, which also contains other methods for training the dog to make those blind retrieves. It's best to teach this with a whistle, and for a Lab, it's best to limit his range to 15 yards in front and 25 yards to either side.

Why limit a pointing dog to spaniel or flushing-dog range? Because pheasants are unpredictable. They may hold, run, or fly. If they flush prematurely, it's a rare hunter who won't shoot just because his dog didn't get a point. If the average hunter's dog, for whatever reason, accidentally flushes the bird, he'll cuss less if his dog—and the bird—are within shotgun range.

Won't shooting over accidental flushes encourage more of the same? Yes, and a great many Labs had very short careers as pointers for that very reason. Their masters couldn't resist shooting a flushed bird that hadn't been pointed. Maybe their owners even encouraged flushing. It only takes a few times before a Lab simply stops pointing.

For this reason, it's extremely important that a pointing Lab be taught to stop-to-flush. (See Step 24.) When a dog stops to flush, you know the flush is accidental. Deliberate flushes are followed by chase. If your dog is minding his manners and stops, you can safely shoot the bird without encouraging flushing and destroying his pointing instincts.

To date, owners have reported the pointing instinct manifesting itself in Labs anywhere from 10 weeks of age to the first hunting season. At this time, it's doubtful that the instinct is strong enough that one might test litters for pups that point as can be done with pointers, setters, and so on. So far, pointing has usually shown up the first time the Lab suddenly slams into hot, strong bird scent—and that's a good way to introduce a Lab's first birds.

Make the scent strong. Hide a box of birds, not just one. If it's pigeons, spray pheasant scent on them as well. Choose a day with good, steady wind drift, not gusty or too strong. Bring the pup across the wind so he'll be only 5 or 10 yards downwind from the birds when the scent hits him like a blast in both nostrils. If his instinct has manifested itself, he'll point.

The training sequence I think best for a pointing Lab is:

1. Name recognition with rewards.
2. Nose awakening.
3. WHOA instead of SIT at the food bowl.
4. Early quartering, quickly leading into use of the whistle.
5. Introduction to water as soon as it's warm enough.
6. Sight fetching in water.
7. Fetching scented-dummy blinds on land.
8. Hunting scented dummies planted to maintain a quartering range of 25 yards to either side and 15 to the front.
9. Introduce gunfire during water fetches, starting with .22 shot shells in a rifle. Fire as you throw the dummy, and follow immediately with FETCH. Work up to the shotgun.
10. When the dog seems ready by pointing a rag (or when you'd just like to test him on live birds), plant the box of birds as I described. He's accustomed to gunfire, so if he points, flush a bird, and kill it for him to fetch. Practice this twice a week to strengthen points. Work down from a box of birds to just one planted at a time to improve his nose work.
11. If the pup is less than 6 months old when his first season opens, hunt alone, and *don't shoot an accidental flush.* If you can't trust yourself not to shoot an accidental flush, leave the dog at home.
12. Teach stop-to-flush.
13. At 8 months or older, teach WHOA, starting on the drum and continuing as with any other bird dog.

If your Lab has the pointing instinct, you'll have a great pheasant dog that also works well on grouse or quail. In fact, if you like, steps 12 and 13, properly taught, can train your Lab to stop and *stand* for birds, even if he doesn't have the instinct to point.

Address Appendix

Bill Boatman & Co.
215 S. Washington St.
Greenfield, OH 45123
Phone: 513/981-7788

Dogs Unlimited
P.O. Box 1844
Chillicothe, OH 45601
Phone: 614/772-2000

Hulme Sporting Goods
P.O. Box 670
Paris, TN 38242
Phone: 901/642-6400

Inter-Cal Corporation
421 Miller Valley Rd.
Prescott, AZ 86301
Phone: 602/445-8063

Leon Measures
408 Fair St.
Livingston, TX 77351
Phone: 713/457-1250

Master's Voice
1415 Danbury Ct.
Belleville, IL 62223
Phone: 800/520-8463 ext. 00

Nite Lite Co.
P.O. Box 1
Clarksville, AR 72830
Phone: 501/754-2146

Pointing Labs
Mayo Kellogg Kennels
RR3 Box 120
Madison, SD 57042
Phone: 605/256-3496

Sporting Dog Specialties
Spencerport, NY 14559
Phone: 716/352-1232

T. E. Scott Co.
10329 Rockville Rd.
Indianapolis, IN 46234
Phone: 317/271-2482

Wick Outdoor Works
Hwy. 19 South
Montgomery City, MO 63361
Phone: 314/564-2201